COMEMOS

COMEMOS

PLANT-FORWARD RECIPES
CELEBRATING CONTEMPORARY
MEXICAN CUISINE

ALEJANDRA GRAF
Creator of ALECOOKS and PILONCILLO&VAINILLA

Gibbs Smith

First Edition
30 29 28 27 26 5 4 3 2 1

Published by
Gibbs Smith
Layton, Utah
www.gibbs-smith.com

The authorized representative in the EEA is Simon & Schuster Netherlands BV, Herculesplein 96 3584 AA Utrecht, Netherlands, info@simonandschuster.nl

Designed by Sheryl Dickert
Library of Congress Control Number: 2026933148
ISBN: 978-1-4236-6947-0
Ebook ISBN: 978-1-4236-6948-7

Printed and bound in China using FSC®-certified and other controlled materials.

FSC
www.fsc.org
MIX
Paper | Supporting responsible forestry
FSC® C144853

To Sergio,

Santiago, Sofia, and Romina—my all.

CONTENTS

INTRODUCTION

I was born in Mexico City; my mom is from Sinaloa, a northwestern state in Mexico, and my dad's family is from Mexico City. For many years, his grandpa, a German man, lived in the state of Hidalgo, a well-known place for eating carnitas. I am married to an American whose mother is from the border (Matamoros and Brownsville, Texas) and whose father is from Veracruz. Over the years, I've had the opportunity to travel and visit family throughout Mexico, and we share one thing: how we approach food.

In our minds, Mexican food and sharing at our table always take center stage. It doesn't matter if it is lunch or a weekday dinner; we always cherish moments together at the table. If we want to celebrate a birthday, we have *una comidita* (meaning the act of preparing something special for a group of people or special person); for a graduation party, we host a big feast; or simply for the joy of sharing a good conversation with a friend or catching up with someone we haven't seen in a long time, we plan to have breakfast or a nice meal together. In essence, food in Mexico isn't just about sustenance. It is an enduring symbol of our culture, history, and, most importantly, our love for one another.

Food is not merely about feeding our bodies; it also nourishes our souls. And what better way to do it than in a relaxed, friendly manner—the Mexican way. A true Mexican thinks, breathes, and loves food.

I used to get annoyed when people referred to Mexican culture as fiestas, siestas, margaritas, chips, and salsas. But lately, it fills my heart to know that this sentiment has evolved; Mexican food and culture have been getting this incredible hype. Mexico City is now a must-visit place on many people's travel lists. I especially love the new interest in Mexican food and modern Mexican flavors.

I assert that for Mexicans, food is an expression of love, a trait woven into our DNA. From ancient civilizations offering food as tribute to their gods to contemporary families preparing meals for their loved ones, our passion for food remains undiminished.

As a child, I recall my mother, grandmother, and aunts discussing new recipes they'd discovered or dishes they wanted to create. Now, as an adult, I look forward to sharing my latest salsa recipe with my siblings or listening to them recount the joy of a recent meal or a newly found restaurant. This approach to food is a love language, a testament to our familial bonds. For us, nothing surpasses the joy of a long "sobremesa," nibbling on Besos de Pistache (page 170) or Pistachio Mazapán (page 169) while sipping a glass of rich red wine or a Carajillo Shakeado (page 186).

Our focus on food is so intense that Fridays have become a day for camaraderie in Mexico City. Known as "Viernes Chilango," this tradition centers on sharing lunch with friends and skipping the afternoon work hours.

This cookbook is all about recipes that can be used during the week or for weekend gatherings. Recipes that bring families together, recipes you want to cook and share with your loved ones, no matter what diet each follows. My cookbook isn't a story handed down from a grandmother or parent. It reflects who we are as Mexicans and what I, a Mexican, can contribute to the food world.

It emphasizes how we approach food, how we sit, eat, and savor every bite, every story shared around the table, and how we cherish time with each person present. It is about enjoying long weekend breakfasts that start with coffee and pan dulce, followed by chilaquiles, and ending with coffee and pan dulce (yes, again). This is the Mexican way. It is about ensuring there is always enough to share, keeping our doors open for family and friends, and always having an extra seat at the table for those who may come. In Mexico, we say that everyone is welcome to our table; we just need to add more water to the beans. And by this philosophy, I grew up and run my household.

It is not strange to get an impromptu invitation from us or receive one from my family and friends. A typical Mexican will say, "Stay for dinner, let's make a quick pasta or *una botanita*, to catch up and enjoy this moment." But this state of mind is not just for an impromptu dinner or an unexpected guest; it is a way of being.

I still remember the moments from my childhood in Mexico City when friends invited me to lunch at their homes. We dined with the whole family on a pretty, well-set table, and there was always enough food for everyone—dishes catering to various tastes and dietary needs. One for vegetarians, one "original," one with specific ingredients, and one without. At my parents' friends-and-family get-togethers or *taquizas*, there was always a meat dish, along with rice, beans, and a vegetable option, among others. There was something for every palate, and the menu was thoughtfully planned with inclusion in mind.

I followed a vegan diet for eighteen years, and now, with adult kids in tow and a very Mexican way of eating, I noticed that my diet was creating conflict with my non-vegan family; the kids started eating out a lot more often, cooking barbecues and carnes asadas in their friends' homes, or skipping dinner altogether. Which, for me, as a Mexican mom, killed me. So I decided to take my eighteen years of experience as a plant-based cook and all the moments that formed my relationship with food as a kid and start cooking dishes for all, dishes that returned us to the table as a family, dishes that are adaptable for my very meat-focused eater Santiago, my foodie daughter with an exemplary palate Sofia, or my curios and *antojada* (craving something all the time) girl Romina.

I started each recipe with a plant-forward foundation, then added options so everyone could make the dish their own. These are the recipes you'll find in this book. Many start out vegan or vegetarian, but they're meant to be customized, not limited. For example, with Three Chiles Chilaquiles (page 67), you can keep them plant-based with cashew crema and tofu, or make them more traditional with real crema, cotija, a fried egg, maybe shredded chicken, or even carne asada. In other recipes, I suggest using mushrooms, plant-based meats, or regular meat, so each dish fits what people like. The base is always flavorful and intentional, but there's room to adjust. It's not about labels or rules—it's about bringing people together. I want to show that vegetarian and vegan food can be abundant, varied, and very flavorful.

As a Mexican, I affirm that our culture's most expressive love language is the art of nourishing one another through food. The table and the kitchen are the heart of our gatherings, where we reconnect, share stories, and celebrate our lives. When we say *comemos* (let's eat, or we eat), it signifies more than just dining; it is an experience that unites us in a sacred moment of communion, unity, and love.

The book's chapters are divided into moments that shape our lifestyle. In them, you'll find recipes created with dietary options in mind. The first chapter is Desayunos (breakfast), followed by Botanas (starters, appetizers) and La Comida, where I share recipes for lunch, dinner, and everything in between, including *meriendas* (a light meal between lunch and dinner), Para El Fin, for the weekend (recipes that take longer to make or are meant to be shared as family style), Sobremesa (time spent at the table after dinner eating sweets), and Bebidas (drinks).

The recipes are easy to follow; some take a bit more time to prepare, but my goal is to have easy, delicious food at the table to share with kids, partners, or any loved ones. With this book, I aim to provide you with tools and options for people to gather at the table every day. I was lucky enough to have dinner with my family every single day, sometimes just the five of us and often with guests, my father's business partners, etc. It was during those moments, at the dinner table, that everything happened—the jokes, the lessons, and the memories. The recipes in this book are the ones I cook to gather with my family, the dishes I crave, and the dishes my kids crave. But more than that, I want everyone to crave that special moment we all experience when we share our meals around the table.

You will find that some ingredients are repeated throughout the book but are cooked differently, or you may find that some dishes can be used in many different ways. This is Mexican cooking at its core! If you have some form of masa element, a guisado, and salsa, you have a meal. Most recipes have various options, meaning you can add eggs or shredded chicken, pork, or beef to make the dish more substantial. I want you to feel free to modify, add, or swap as you wish; I want you to make these bold Mexican recipes your own.

ESSENTIAL TOOLS

I am a minimalist when it comes to kitchen tools, valuing the basics like a good knife, a tortilla press, a sturdy cutting board, and bowls of various sizes. However, I firmly believe that it's worth investing in a beautiful pot, a quality blender, and aesthetically pleasing, functional tools. When I cook in a light, calming space with beautiful tools, I create lovely dishes, and I feel happy to be in and return to this sacred space.

The same goes for ingredients; starting with beautiful and flavorful components leads to a delicious and appetizing dish. As much as I love shopping and visiting a good grocery store, I prefer to buy the essentials and maintain control over my cooking. So, I do not buy pre-seasoned ingredients or spice mixes (no taco mix here!). Yet, as a busy mom, I also appreciate the convenience of a can of beans or frozen vegetables.

Braiser

A cast-iron braiser is good to have, but it is not necessary; you can definitely use a skillet instead. Mine is a hand-me-down from my mom, and I love to cook Picadillo (page 128), Cortadillo (page 131), and Tinga (page 132) using it.

A good knife and a sturdy cutting board

The first time I bought a chef's knife was a complete disaster. I cut myself, tried using it on flimsy plastic cutting boards that slid around every time I made a cut, and quickly realized I had no idea what I was doing. I had to take a step back, educate myself, and actually learn about knives and cutting boards. I'm saving you from that hassle.

Here's what I learned and what I use every day. Invest in one heavy, large, sturdy wooden cutting board for most of your everyday cooking: onions, garlic, potatoes, carrots, and all your general prep. Then keep a second, lighter cutting board made from a nonporous, dishwasher-safe material specifically for proteins. Look for one with silicone corners or a nonslip edge. If it doesn't have that, simply place a damp kitchen towel or paper towel underneath to keep it from moving. It makes a huge difference for safety, confidence, and joy in the kitchen.

When it comes to knives, I also quickly realized I didn't need a full set, that less was more. I could do everything with just three good knives. For your main workhorse, the one that handles most of the chopping, I recommend a 7- to 9-inch chef's knife. It's worth shopping for in person if you can, so you can feel the weight, balance, and how it sits in your hand. A knife should feel comfortable and steady in your palm, not awkward or heavy in the wrong way.

Alongside that, I always recommend a small paring knife for quick jobs like peeling, trimming, and detail work, and one serrated knife for bread, tomatoes, and anything with a tough exterior and soft interior. I also love having a good pair of kitchen scissors on hand.

They're very useful, especially when working with dried chiles, cutting them open, removing stems, or trimming them into pieces before toasting or soaking.

Large Dutch oven

A large Dutch oven is always perfect for cooking beans from scratch or boiling pasta. What I love about them is that you can start the recipe on the stove and move it to the oven without a thought. I recommend an 8-quart pot.

Mason jars

My favorite way to store cremas, salsas, and pickled onions. These are inexpensive, easy to wash, and come in a great variety of sizes. If you can, buy them with plastic lids.

Microplane

If you don't have one, I really want to encourage you to buy one. Lime zest is a star in many recipes, so it is good to have a Microplane on hand. Besides, I promise you will use it nonstop to zest oranges and lemons, and even grate Parmesan cheese.

Mixing bowls

All sizes because you will be cooking up a storm, promise.

Rimmed baking sheets

Half-sheet and quarter-pan sheets are great to have. You will need them to bake all the cookies and roast vegetables. I love to line them with precut parchment paper; it not only makes them easier to clean but also makes them nonstick.

Serving platters

This is not a formal tool, but I highly encourage you to buy extended platters or large, shallow bowls. These are perfect for serving pasta and salad in a family-style setting.

Skillets

One large and one small—yes, it is that simple, only for pans: One 10- to 12-inch and one 6- to 8-inch pan. I do like ones with a lid. If they don't come with a lid, you can always get a universal or silicone one. I recommend buying the best that you can afford. I love stainless steel and ceramic nonstick pans.

Tortilla press

Before I tell you about a good tortilla press, I must confess that I grew up eating freshly made tortillas, from griddle to mouth, del comal a la boca, as we say in Mexico. But I did not know how to make them until recently. I have a regular round tortilla press, but my favorite is an Oaxacan one. These are square, colorful, and heavy. I highly recommend making your tortillas at home; I promise you'll never go back to store-bought ones, or if you do, you'll definitely seek out better tortillas. Mine is from Masienda.

Wooden spoons and silicone spatulas, whisks and kitchen tongs

Don't be shy and have a lot of these tools. They make cooking easy and more enjoyable. When you have the right tools, everything works better in every area of your life. Don't you think?

ESSENTIAL INGREDIENTS

Where to buy Mexican ingredients

Please don't think that getting dried chiles is the hardest thing in the world. Nowadays, it is very easy to get good-quality ingredients online, and many of my favorite shops can even deliver to your home.

Corn tortillas

Please, please, please, if you don't make them yourself with good masa harina, buy ones with minimal ingredients. A good corn tortilla should have corn, water, and lime—no extra anything. Also, if you can find organic tortillas in the supermarkets' refrigerators, those are even better. For store-bought tortillas, I recommend Masienda, and Yoli Tortillería.

Dried chiles and spices

To tell you the truth, I buy my dried chiles and spices from Amazon. I prefer to purchase small quantities and store them in mason jars in my pantry. The ones I use the most are guajillo, ancho, and chile de árbol. When buying dried chiles, look for ones with even color and pliable skin, not brittle.

Mole

I don't make my mole because there are delicious moles ready to eat. I recommend authentic mole sauces like the ones from Hernán (hernanmexico.com), I Love Mole (store.ilovemole.com), and Ya Oaxaca (yaoaxaca.com).

Produce

Roma tomatoes are the best for Mexican food. Mexican food typically features two types of onions: white and red. Red onions are usually used to garnish dishes, while white (or yellow) onions are used for cooking. I buy my produce everywhere. I don't have a preference as long as it is fresh and properly ripened, but I always remember that if I start with incredibly ripe and high-quality produce, I will end up with a much better and tastier dish.

Always on hand: white and yellow onions, red onion, and garlic.

Limes. The acidity of a lime is precisely what you need for a Mexican dish.

Fresh herbs and chiles. Having fresh herbs on hand makes all the difference in a dish—it's that extra layer of flavor that brings everything to life. I always try to keep cilantro and mint in my refrigerator. Cilantro is my go-to for anything Mexican: tacos, salsas, soups—you name it. And mint? It's surprisingly versatile. I use it in aguas frescas, salads, gorditas, etc.

As for chiles, I treat them like flavor gold. A couple of fresh serranos or jalapeños go a long way. They don't just bring heat—they add depth, brightness, and a whole lot of personality.

Once you start cooking with fresh herbs and chiles regularly, it's hard to go back.

Salsa macha

You will want to add the Mexican chili oil to everything—from quesadillas to the Pasta con Salsa Macha (page 157), to everything. In the next chapter, you will find my very easy, unconventional way to make salsa macha, which is incredibly delicious. If you're not ready to create your own, using a store-bought one is no problem.

Salt

I always use Diamond Crystal kosher salt. This is very important, because I developed all my recipes using this type of salt. Do yourself a favor and order a big box of it online. I promise you won't regret it. This salt gives you more control over the overall seasoning of each dish. If you use table salt or sea salt, use half of what is recommended in each recipe. Finishing salts give the dish a restaurant-style experience of a salty punch with each bite. I love using Maldon Salt or Sal de Colima, which is a natural and unprocessed salt from the state of Colima in Mexico. While you can use Sal de Colima as a regular salt, I prefer to use it as a finishing salt.

Vegan substitutions

All of the cheeses in these recipes can be replaced with plant-based alternatives. Use Violife block cheeses for shredding or slicing, and choose a vegan ricotta such as Kite Hill for a creamy, bake-friendly texture. For sour cream, Follow Your Heart makes a reliable option. For mayonnaise, use Hellmann's Vegan or Follow Your Heart Vegenaise. If butter is needed, Miyoko's cultured vegan butter works especially well for both cooking and baking.

LOS BÁSICOS

THE BASICS

This chapter is about salsas, dressings, beans, and rice—everything you need in your pantry and fridge to make a quick meal. I will give you the Mexican framework so you can think of it as one when reading this chapter.

We always have tortillas, a good salsa, rice, and beans in the refrigerator.

From there, you can create magic. Imagine having a good salsa verde and corn tortillas; the easiest thing to do is make quesadillas. But if you don't feel like cooking dinner, make migas with a side of beans (any type of beans), all topped with salsa verde. Or make bean and cheese quesadillas. I am not a nutritionist or registered dietitian, but as a mom, I know that we have protein, good carbs, and veggies in there. Some of these salsas are meant to be made once a week and kept in the refrigerator until ready to use. I designed them to enhance a meal. For example, if you make a quesadilla and add pico de gallo or guacamole, you're set. Or a tostada with refried beans and salsa is already a perfect lunch.

SALSA ROJA DE TODOS LOS DÍAS

Every-Single-Day Salsa

I can guarantee that you'll find a container with a good salsa whenever you open a Mexican family's refrigerator. Every family has its recipe and different levels of spiciness. Growing up at my parents' house, the salsa roja had only tomatoes and chiles; my cousin's salsa has roasted tomatillos and lime juice. Here is my household salsa recipe. I want to share it with you, and I hope you have it in your refrigerator as I do and use it on everything, from quesadillas to tacos to grilled proteins.

MAKES ABOUT 2 CUPS

4 Roma tomatoes

¼ small white onion

2 garlic cloves (unpeeled)

2 to 4 serrano chiles (adjust to taste)

1 teaspoon kosher salt, plus more as needed

Heat a comal, skillet, or griddle over medium-high heat. Place the tomatoes, onion, garlic, and serrano chiles. Roast them, turning occasionally, until they're nicely charred and softened, 10 to 15 minutes.

Once charred, peel the garlic and transfer all the ingredients to a blender. Add the salt and blend until smooth or pulse to make it slightly chunky, depending on your preference.

Taste the salsa and add more salt if needed.

NOTES

- *Serve with tacos, quesadillas, rice bowls, or just tortilla chips.*
- *If you want to make it spicier, add more serrano chiles; if you want to make it less spicy, use jalapeño peppers instead.*
- *Store in an airtight jar in the refrigerator; it lasts up to 1 week.*

SALSA VERDE

Authentic Salsa Verde

When you go to any Mexican restaurant, you always get different salsas at the center of the table, which is also very common in Mexican households. Growing up, even before we sat at the table, there was always a piece of queso panela (some type of fresh cheese) that my mom bought from Mexico City even though we lived in Monterrey, agua fresca (it all depended on which fruit was in season), freshly made tortillas, and two types of salsa, one extra spicy for my siblings and one barely spicy for the rest of us. This salsa verde is one of them; make it as spicy as you want by adding more serranos.

MAKES ABOUT 2 CUPS

5 to 7 tomatillos, depending on the size

1 to 2 serrano chile peppers

¼ small white onion

1 garlic clove

1 teaspoon kosher salt

¾ cup water

1 cup cilantro leaves and stems, tightly packed

Remove the husks from the tomatillos and rinse them thoroughly until clean. Remove the stems from the chiles. Place the tomatillos, chiles, onion, garlic, and salt into a small saucepan with the water. Cover the saucepan and cook for 10 to 15 minutes, until the tomatillos change color to a very pale green and begin to soften.

Using a slotted spoon, transfer the vegetables to a blender and discard the cooking water Add the cilantro and blend everything together until smooth. Taste the mixture and adjust the seasoning as needed.

SALSA VERDE CRUDA

Raw Salsa Verde

This is one of my favorite salsa recipes of all time. I remember eating it as a kid, a teenager, and an adult, and it's always blown my mind how the combination of four simple ingredients can give a burst of brightness, happiness, and flavor to everything you put it on.

This salsa is perfect with chilaquiles, fried masa quesadillas, and everything. You'll see. And on top of it all, it is the simplest thing to do EVER. Everything goes straight into the blender—no cooking is needed.

MAKES ABOUT 2 CUPS

¼ small white or yellow onion

5 tomatillos

1 bunch cilantro, coarsely chopped

1 serrano chile pepper or more to taste

1 teaspoon kosher salt

Peel and coarsely cut the onion. Remove the husks from the tomatillos and rinse them under running water to remove the sticky residue; then, coarsely chop them.

Add the cilantro, onion, tomatillos, and chile pepper (you can remove the seeds if you want it less spicy) to a blender. Sprinkle in the salt. Blend until you achieve the desired consistency. Taste and adjust the salt if needed. Serve immediately or store in the refrigerator for a few hours to let the flavors come together even more.

NOTES

- *Blend in an avocado to make it creamier, chop all the ingredients to make it chunkier, or blend the salsa ingredients and finish it with chopped avocado. Every combination works.*
- *Add the cilantro at the end if you find it sticks to your blender blade.*
- *This salsa is meant to be eaten the day it's made.*

SALSA MACHA DE AJONJOLÍ Y PEPITAS

Mexican Sesame and Pumpkin Seeds Chili Crisp

First, I must share that this is the kind of salsa I could enjoy by the spoonful every single day, no matter the time! I truly adore the rich complexity of the flavors and textures. In a strange way, I think of it as a little piece of Mexico captured in a jar. To me, Mexico embodies complexity. It's vibrant, busy, and brimming with wonderful things!

In the book, you'll see I call for salsa macha in different recipes. This is my favorite recipe I've ever developed for salsa macha, and not only because it is delicious but also because I made it super simple to prepare.

MAKES ABOUT 4 CUPS

4 chiles de árbol

6 guajillo chiles

6 pasilla chiles

¾ cup toasted sesame seeds

¾ cup pepitas and/or sunflower seeds

2 teaspoons kosher salt or 1 teaspoon sea salt

1 teaspoon Mexican oregano

1 teaspoon garlic powder

1 tablespoon apple cider vinegar

1½ cup vegetable oil (add ½ cup if you like a more oil-based salsa)

Start by removing the stems from the dried chiles and discarding them. Then, using a high-speed blender or food processor, add the chiles and pulse until they are very finely chopped—almost pulverized. Blend the chiles in batches to avoid overloading your machine for best results.

Add the sesame seeds and pepitas to a large glass jar with a wide mouth or a stainless steel or glass bowl. Once the chiles are ready, add them to the pepita and sesame seed mixture. Stir in the salt, oregano, and garlic, then pour in the vinegar and mix well.

Please be careful in this next step. Heat the oil over medium heat in a stainless-steel saucepan until just before it begins to shimmer. Turn off the heat and carefully pour the hot oil over the seed and chile mixture. Very carefully mix with a wooden spoon and let it sit and cool for 10 to 15 minutes, or until it's cool enough to handle.

Taste and adjust the seasoning if needed. Once completely cooled, store the salsa macha in a tightly closed jar in the refrigerator, for 2 to 3 weeks.

NOTES

- *If it's your first time making salsa macha, use a large bowl and allow everything to cool completely before tasting or serving.*
- *If you prefer your salsa to be less spicy, remove the seeds from the chiles and reduce the amount of chiles de árbol, which are the spiciest.*
- *You can use toasted or raw sesame, pepita, or sunflower seeds; I do prefer toasted, though.*

CHILES EN VINAGRE

Mexican Pickled Jalapeños

Jalapeños are fantastic; they are crunchy, spicy, and delightful. Mexican pickled jalapeños are truly a dream come true, with each slice of chile or pickled vegetable adding the perfect flavor boost to everything you put on it. In Mexico, we add them to quesadillas, burritas (a quesadilla made with ham, cheese, and two tortillas), tortas, sandwiches, and even popcorn. If you ever go to the cinema in Mexico, I guarantee you'll find someone preparing their palomitas (popcorn) with jalapeño slices and brine.

MAKES ABOUT 4 CUPS

3 tablespoons vegetable or olive oil

2 cups peeled and cut into rounds carrots

1 large onion, thinly sliced

1 whole garlic head, halved (skin on)

1 pound jalapeño peppers, halved or sliced (remove seeds for less heat)

3 to 4 cups white vinegar (enough to cover the vegetables)

1 bay leaf

1 teaspoon dried thyme

1 teaspoon dried oregano (preferably Mexican oregano)

1 teaspoon dried marjoram, optional

¼ teaspoon whole peppercorns

1 teaspoon kosher salt

Heat the oil in a nonreactive pot (glass, stainless steel, or enameled cast iron) over medium heat. Add the carrots and sauté for 3 to 4 minutes. Add the onion, the garlic head halves, and jalapeños. Sauté another 2 to 3 minutes until just softened; do not brown.

Pour in the vinegar until the vegetables are covered. Add the bay leaf, thyme, oregano, marjoram (if using), peppercorns, and salt. Bring to a gentle simmer.

Simmer for 5 to 10 minutes, stirring occasionally, until the jalapeños turn from bright green to a dull, dark green. Remove from the heat and let cool.

Once cooled, transfer the vegetables to clean glass jars, ensuring they are fully submerged in the liquid, removing any loose garlic skins. Close the jars with lids and refrigerate.

NOTES

- *Depending on how they are prepared and stored, Chiles en Vinagre can last several weeks to several months in the refrigerator.*
- *To ensure maximum freshness and flavor, store them in an airtight container in the refrigerator and consume them within a few weeks of opening.*

CEBOLLAS EN VINAGRE

Mexican Pickled Onions

I must've been born a vegetarian foodie—there's just no other explanation. Growing up, whenever my parents hosted dinner parties, cochinita pibil was often the star of the table: that slow-roasted pork from Yucatán served in tacos with Mexican pickled onions and habanero salsa. But little me? I skipped the meat. I'd pile warm tortillas with just the pickled onions or smear them with refried black beans and top them with a generous spoonful of those tangy, spicy onions and sauce. To this day, I'm still obsessed with that crunch, that acidity, that burst of brightness they bring to every dish. This recipe is my forever go-to for making Mexican pickled onions at home. They are simple, bold, and full of childhood memories.

MAKES ABOUT 2½ TO 3 CUPS

1 cup water

1 cup white vinegar

1 bay leaf

1 tablespoon kosher salt, plus more as needed

5 black peppercorns

2 teaspoons Mexican oregano

2 medium red onions, thinly sliced (about 3½ loosely packed cups)

Juice of 2 large limes

In a medium saucepan, combine the water, vinegar, bay leaf, salt, peppercorns, and oregano. Bring to a boil over medium-high heat. As soon as it boils, remove from the heat and immediately add the sliced onions, pressing them down so they are fully submerged.

Let them sit until completely cooled. As they rest, the onions will soften, shrink in volume, and take on a pink hue.

Discard the liquid and transfer the onions to a clean glass jar or container. Stir in the lime juice and add a pinch of salt, if needed. The flavor should be bright and slightly punchy. Taste and adjust seasoning as necessary.

I like to leave the peppercorns and bay leaf in the jar for extra flavor, but you may remove them if you prefer. Store the onions in a tightly sealed jar in the refrigerator for up to 2 weeks.

PICO DE GALLO

This is a fresh and classic Mexican pico de gallo made with ripe tomatoes, onion, cilantro, and chile. Perfect as a topping for tacos, molletes, or any dish that needs a dash of freshness. Add lime juice if you like, but it's not always necessary!

This salsa is perfect freshly made, but it doesn't store well, so it is best to only prepare the amount you need.

MAKES ABOUT 2 ½ CUPS

4 ripe Roma tomatoes, diced

½ medium white onion, finely chopped

1 serrano or jalapeño chile, finely diced

¼ cup chopped cilantro

Kosher salt

1 tablespoon olive oil

Lime juice, optional (for extra brightness)

Place the tomatoes, onion, chile, and cilantro in a medium bowl.

Season with salt to taste, then drizzle with olive oil. Gently stir to combine. Squeeze in lime juice (if using).

Let it sit for 10 to 15 minutes, if possible, to allow the flavors to meld. Taste and adjust with more salt if needed. Serve immediately.

NOTES

- *Skip the lime juice for a more traditional taste.*
- *For a spicier salsa, keep the chile seeds and veins; remove them for a milder version.*
- *This is best served fresh but can be stored in an airtight container in the refrigerator for up to 2 days. Drain excess liquid before serving. Do not freeze—the texture changes significantly after thawing.*

GUACAMOLE

I truly believe that no Mexican cookbook would be complete without guacamole! As my good friend likes to say, avocados are truly the Mexican butter. So having a delightful guac recipe is essential to this book. At home, we enjoy it so much, using it with everything, which makes it one of those recipes I'm excited to share with you. In fact, as I mentioned in the introduction, I've had the joy of living in both the central and northern parts of Mexico, and with family scattered all over the country, I'm thrilled to share with you my three favorite guacamole recipes I've gathered. Guacamole is best enjoyed the day you make it, as it doesn't keep well.

Guacamole con Limoncito
Guacamole with Lime

MAKES 2½ TO 3 CUPS

4 ripe avocados

½ cup diced yellow or white onion

1 serrano chile pepper or 2 jalapeños, finely chopped (seeds removed for less heat)

1 teaspoon kosher salt

Juice of 3 small limes

½ bunch of cilantro, chopped (about ½ cup packed)

Cut the avocados in half, remove the pits, and scoop the flesh into a bowl. Using a fork or potato masher, mash the avocados to your desired consistency, chunky or smooth. Stir in the diced onion, chopped chile, and salt. Pour in the lime juice and mix well. Fold in the chopped cilantro and taste for seasoning. Add more salt or lime juice if needed. Enjoy immediately.

Guacamole de mi Casa
Guacamole from My Kitchen

MAKES 2 TO 2½ CUPS

1 small garlic clove

4 ripe avocados

Juice of 2 to 3 small limes (adjust to taste)

1 teaspoon kosher salt (adjust to taste)

Peel the garlic and smash it in a molcajete or use a garlic press. Cut the avocados in half, remove the pits, and scoop the flesh into a bowl. Mash with a fork to form a paste. Stir in the garlic, lime juice, and salt. Mix everything and taste. Add more lime or salt if needed.

NOTE

- *If you find the raw garlic flavor too strong, try this: Add the lime juice and salt directly to the minced garlic, then let it sit for about 5 minutes. This softens the sharpness, and then you can mix it into the mashed avocados.*

Guacamole Bandera
Mexican Flag Guacamole

MAKES 3 TO 3½ CUPS

4 ripe avocados

½ teaspoon kosher salt

Juice of 2 limes

1 cup diced tomato (Roma or vine-ripe)

¼ cup finely chopped white or red onion

¼ cup chopped fresh cilantro

1 jalapeño or serrano chile pepper, finely chopped (remove seeds for less heat)

In a large bowl, scoop out the avocado flesh and mash it to your desired texture. Season the avocado with the salt and lime juice. Transfer to a serving bowl and, with a spatula, smooth out the top. Layer the vegetables, arranging one row of each color: tomatoes, onions, then cilantro and chile. The goal is to mix everything at the table or to scoop up a bit of each vegetable with each bite.

TAJÍN HECHO EN CASA

Homemade Tajín

Here's a little secret: I'm a huge fan of store-bought Tajín. It's my go-to for its convenience, availability, and that unbeatable acidity. But there are moments when I need a homemade version, either because I've run out or I'm craving something less tangy. That's when my own Tajín recipe steps in. It's perfect for sprinkling over oranges or veggies or as a drink rim, and it's a delightful twist on homemade popcorn.

MAKES ½ CUP

2 tablespoons ground ancho chile

1 teaspoon ground chile seco (like guajillo, árbol, or a mild dried red chile)

1 tablespoon ground dehydrated lime zest or citric acid

2 teaspoons kosher salt

1 teaspoon granulated sugar

Mix the ingredients together in a bowl and then store in an airtight container. It will last up to 4 months. Like other spices, it won't go bad—it will just lose its freshness over time.

NOTE

- *If you want it to be more acidic, add an extra teaspoon of citric acid. You can find it in the spice section.*

CREMA DE CASHEWS

Cashew Mexican Crema

This simple, tangy cashew sauce is perfect for drizzling over bowls, tacos, or using as a dip. It's dairy-free, ultra-creamy, and easy to customize.

MAKES ABOUT 1½ CUPS

1 cup raw, unsalted cashews

¾ cup water, plus more for soaking and as needed

2 tablespoons fresh lemon juice

1 tablespoon apple cider vinegar

½ teaspoon kosher salt

Place the cashews in a bowl and cover them with water. Let them soak for at least 1 hour and up to 3 hours. For an even creamier texture, soak overnight in the refrigerator.

After soaking, drain and rinse the cashews well.

Add the soaked cashews to a high-speed blender along with the ¾ cup water, lemon juice, vinegar, and salt. Blend on high until completely smooth and creamy. Scrape down the sides as needed.

Taste and adjust salt or acidity if needed. For a thinner consistency, add a splash more water and blend again.

NOTE

- *Store in an airtight container in the refrigerator for up to 5 days. It may thicken as it sits; just stir in a little water to loosen it up.*

ARROZ BLANCO

Mexican White Rice

Fluffy, flavorful, and the perfect side dish for your favorite Mexican meals, this is a favorite of mine. I love to keep a container in my refrigerator with rice. If I have rice, beans, a good salsa, and tortillas in the refrigerator, I can make magic for dinner. Think Chiles Poblanos en Hojaldre con Arroz, Crema, y Queso (page 124), rice and beans, or Enchiladas Suizas Rojas (page 126), or you can crisp the rice up and add it to a salad.

MAKES 3 CUPS

1 cup long-grain white rice

1 tablespoon vegetable oil or butter

¼ medium white onion

1 garlic clove

2 teaspoons kosher salt

1 to 2 cups water or vegetable broth, divided

1 to 2 sprigs fresh cilantro

1 whole serrano chile pepper

Rinse the white rice under cold water until the water runs clear. In a large skillet or saucepan, heat the oil over medium-high heat. Add the rice and sauté for about 2 minutes, stirring constantly to toast it evenly and prevent sticking.

In a blender, combine the onion, garlic, salt, and 1 cup of water. Blend until smooth. You should get about 1½ cups of liquid. Add the remaining 1 cup water to reach a total of 2 cups.

Carefully pour the blended liquid into the pan with the rice. Stir to combine. Add the cilantro sprigs and the whole chile on top.

Cover the pan and reduce the heat to low. Cook the rice for 15 minutes, without lifting the lid.

Turn off the heat and let the rice rest, still covered, for an additional 5 minutes.

Remove the cilantro and chile. Fluff the rice with a fork, taste, and adjust salt if needed. Serve warm.

NOTE

- *This recipe can be doubled without a problem and freezes perfectly. It also turns out great in a rice cooker.*

TOFU QUESO FRESCO

Crumbled Tofu "Queso Fresco"

My journey to veganism began with my son Santiago's dairy allergy. Living in Mexico, our family life revolved around a unique twist on traditional Mexican dishes—a tofu queso fresco. Santiago adored it, and to this day, his love for "tofu quesito" is unwavering, especially when it comes to his favorite chilaquiles.

This plant-based queso fresco alternative, made from tofu, red onion, and salt, is a versatile addition to your collection of recipes. Whether you're finishing or stuffing enchiladas, enmoladas, or entomatadas, this tofu-based cheese substitute is the perfect dairy-free alternative.

MAKES 2¼ TO 2½ CUPS

1 (14-ounce) block firm or extra-firm tofu

¼ to ½ cup finely diced red onion

¾ to 1 teaspoon kosher salt

Wrap the tofu in a clean kitchen towel or paper towels and place a heavy object on top (like a skillet or a few cookbooks). Let it sit for 15 to 30 minutes to remove excess moisture.

Depending on the texture you prefer, cut the tofu into small cubes or gently crumble it with your hands into a bowl.

Add the onion and salt. Gently toss until well combined. Taste and adjust salt as needed. For best flavor, let the mixture rest for 10 to 15 minutes before using, allowing the salt to draw out flavor and the onion to soften slightly.

NOTE

- *For extra tang, add a few drops of lime juice or a pinch of nutritional yeast for a more cheesy flavor.*

FRIJOLITOS REFRITOS CON ACEITE DE OLIVA

Olive Oil Refried Beans

There's this idea that all Mexican food has to be drenched in lard or loaded with fat to be good. But that couldn't be further from the truth. Long before the Spanish arrived, our ancestors cooked with plant-based fats like avocado and seed oils. They didn't have access to lard or olive oil until colonization.

Only after the Spanish introduced pigs and European ingredients did animal fats and olive oil enter our kitchens. But from the beginning, traditional Mexican cooking was rooted in wholesome, plant-based fats. So no, Mexican food doesn't need to be greasy to be authentic. It's always been more balanced and plant-powered than people think.

And yes, I reach for olive oil—it's my favorite, and it's plant-powered, just like the food I love to cook.

MAKES 2½ CUPS

3 tablespoons olive oil

1 medium white or yellow onion, finely diced

3 cups cooked pinto or black beans or 2 (15-ounce) cans of beans, drained

Kosher salt

Heat the olive oil in a large skillet over medium heat. Add the onion and sauté until soft and golden brown.

Add the beans to the pan with a pinch of salt. If they are too dry, add a little vegetable broth or water. Start by adding ¼ cup, then gradually add more if needed.

Using a potato masher or the back of a wooden spoon, mash the beans to the desired consistency. If you prefer softer beans, add a little more water.

Taste the beans and add salt if needed. Simmer for a few more minutes to allow the flavors to blend. Always remember that the beans will thicken when cold.

JARABE DE CAFÉ DE OLLA

Café de Olla Syrup

On one of our last trips to Mexico City, we took the kids to explore the Centro Histórico, where Bellas Artes, the Museo del Templo Mayor, and the main cathedral are. As the kids got older, we decided that every time we visited family in Mexico, we'd set aside a day or two to be tourists in our own city.

And honestly? It's magical. Even for us, being originally from Mexico City, it feels like a completely different experience when you look at it through tourist eyes.

That day, we took the kids to La Churrería El Moro, one of the city's oldest and most iconic spots for churros. My son ordered a café de olla, and the moment he took his first sip, his face lit up. "Mom, why is this the first time I'm trying this? This is amazing!"

That moment stuck with me. And it's what inspired me to create a café de olla syrup so we could re-create that same cozy, spiced flavor back home. We stir it into coffee or drizzle it over oatmeal or pancakes, and sometimes I even bake with it.

MAKES 1 CUP

1 cone (8 ounces) piloncillo (unrefined cane sugar)

1 (2- to 3-inch-long) orange peel piece

2 cinnamon sticks

1 star of anise

5 cloves

1 cup water

Combine the piloncillo, orange peel, and spices in a medium saucepan with the water. Place the saucepan over medium heat and bring the mixture to a simmer. Stir occasionally to help the piloncillo dissolve and to prevent the mixture from sticking to the pan.

Once the piloncillo is fully dissolved, reduce the heat to low. Let the mixture simmer gently for 3 to 5 minutes. Remove the spices and the orange peel and let the syrup cool to room temperature. Transfer the cooled syrup to a clean jar or bottle. You can store it in the refrigerator for up to 1 month.

NOTE

- *Use this syrup over pancakes, as a sweetener for coffee or tea, or to drizzle over buñuelos, churros, or even French toast.*
- *Peel the orange with a vegetable peeler, and make sure to avoid the white pith.*

TORTILLAS DE MAÍZ

Corn Tortillas

There is not much I can say about corn tortillas that does not speak to my love for Mexico, its people, and its food. Every time I heat up one, the smell of it takes me back to my country, to the kitchen of the home I grew up in, where the tortillas were made just when we sat at the table. The comfort of opening the refrigerator and finding a stack of homemade tortillas for quesadillas or other dishes is a feeling that warms my heart.

Now that I live in the United States, a country that I also deeply love, I have to confess it took me a while to learn how to make tortillas. But believe me when I say, the joy of learning this art is unparalleled. Once you learn, there's no turning back. Double or triple the recipe, freeze them, and have a bunch in the refrigerator. If they get a bit old and hard, make migas with them, or cut them up, fry them, and make chilaquiles.

MAKES 16 TORTILLAS

2 cups masa harina

¾ teaspoon kosher salt, optional

1½ cups warm water, plus more as needed

Cut 2 (9-inch) circles or squares from a thin plastic bag or ziplock bag and set aside. In a pinch, you can use parchment paper.

In a large bowl, combine the masa harina and salt (if using). Gradually add the warm water, mixing with your hand until the dough comes together. Knead for about 2 minutes until it feels like soft Play-Doh. Add water or masa harina as needed for consistency.

Cover the dough with a damp kitchen towel and let it rest for 10 or up to 30 minutes to hydrate. If you're short on time, you can start making them right away.

Divide the dough into golf ball–size portions (1 to 2 tablespoons each). Roll into smooth balls and keep covered with a damp towel.

Place a dough ball between the two pieces of plastic bag. Press with a tortilla press (see page 60) or roll gently with a rolling pin into a 6-inch circle about ⅛ inch thick.

Heat a comal, griddle, or skillet over medium-high heat. Ensure it's hot before starting. Place a tortilla on the skillet and cook for 30 seconds on one side. Flip and cook for 1 minute on the second side. Flip again and cook for 30 seconds, pressing gently around the edges with a spatula to encourage puffing.

Transfer cooked tortillas to a tortilla warmer or wrap them in a clean kitchen towel.

Repeat with the remaining dough balls.

NOTES

- *If your first tortillas come out cracked or the edges look rough, your masa is too dry. Add a bit more water. Smooth edges mean you are right where you want to be.*
- *Make sure your comal, griddle, or skillet is hot enough; if not, the tortilla will stick. I like to preheat it for 5 to 8 minutes before making my first tortilla.*
- *Reheat tortillas on a hot skillet for 10 to 15 seconds on each side or in a microwave wrapped in a damp paper towel for 20 to 30 seconds.*
- *Store in the refrigerator wrapped in a dish towel inside a plastic bag, for up to 3 days.*

TOTOPOS

Homemade Corn Chips

Homemade tortillas make chips that are rustic and full of flavor, perfect if you love that from-scratch taste. Just keep in mind—they might puff up a bit if they're very fresh. Store-bought tortillas, on the other hand, deliver more consistent results and are super easy to work with, making them a reliable choice when you need chips in a hurry for your botanas or to make chilaquiles.

MAKES BETWEEN 48 TO 72 TOTOPOS

12 corn tortillas (homemade, page 40, or store-bought)

Neutral oil (like avocado or vegetable oil)

Kosher salt

Dry out the tortillas if they're too soft or fresh by leaving them out for 15 to 30 minutes or by placing them in a slightly warm oven for 5 to 10 minutes. This helps them crisp up better.

Cut tortillas into triangles (quarters or sixths).

Air Fryer Method

Lightly brush or spray both sides of the tortilla pieces with oil.

Place in a single layer, avoid overlapping, in the air fryer basket. Air fry at 350°F (175°C) for 6 to 8 minutes, shaking halfway through. Keep a close eye toward the end to avoid burning.

Sprinkle with salt while warm.

Deep Fryer / Stovetop Frying

Heat 1 to 2 inches of oil in a skillet or deep pan to 350°F (175°C).

Add the tortilla triangles in batches—don't overcrowd. Fry for 1 to 2 minutes, flipping once, until golden and crispy. Remove with a slotted spoon and drain on paper towels.

Salt immediately.

NOTE

- *Homemade tortillas may need an extra minute or two, depending on thickness.*

DESAYUNO

BREAKFAST

In Mexico, we take our breakfasts seriously, especially on the weekends. It's very common to go out for breakfast on Saturdays or Sundays, or to gather with family to celebrate birthdays, christenings, or just being together. And one thing all weekend breakfasts have in common? They're slow, wholesome, and always start with pan dulce and coffee.

When you arrive at a celebration, the first thing they offer isn't the main dish—it's sweet bread. Either someone passes around a plate of conchas and orejas, or there's a basket already waiting at the center of the table. Then comes the coffee, then the orange or green juice, and only after that comes breakfast—chilaquiles, enmoladas, molletes. And of course, after breakfast, you circle back to pan dulce . . . or cake, depending on the occasion.

I know that pace isn't realistic for every day, so in this chapter, I included recipes that cover it all: quick weekday staples like granola, smoothies, and green juice—but also the classics like conchas, garibaldis, and my favorite breakfast ever: chilaquiles.

There are recipes here for everyday mornings and for slow, celebratory breakfasts—even if the celebration is simply being grateful for a quiet weekend or the privilege of waking up next to someone you love. And yes, some of these breakfasts are perfect for lunch . . . or breakfast-for-dinner too.

JUGO VERDE

Mexican Green Juice

In Mexico, ordering a green juice always means getting one made with nopales (cactus paddles). Whenever I prepare this juice at home, it takes my kids back to fond memories of having breakfast with my dad at the country club. He would often take them for a day there during the summer, and breakfast was a ritual. They would always order sunny-side-up eggs with a side of refried beans topped with queso fresco, their green juice, and pan dulce.

This is my take on the green juice; I use my high-speed Vitamix blender, but if you don't have one, a regular blender works fine too—you can just strain the juice afterward.

SERVES 2

1 to 2 nopal cactus paddles, peeled and sliced

1 cup chopped fresh pineapple

1 orange, peeled

3 celery stalks, chopped

1 lime, peeled

2 cups water or coconut water for extra hydration

Place everything in the blender and blend until smooth. If you don't have a high-speed blender and don't like the pulp, strain it using a fine-mesh strainer, an old kitchen towel, or a nut bag.

NOTES

- *Whenever I visit a Mexican supermarket or even just spot fresh nopales at my local grocery store I stock up and freeze them. I do the same with pineapple: Either I buy it already frozen or cut and freeze it myself. This way, I always have the key ingredients ready to make Jugo Verde whenever I crave it.*
- *To keep the pieces from sticking together, line a baking sheet with parchment paper and spread out the pineapple chunks or sliced or whole nopales in a single layer. Freeze until solid, then transfer to a freezer bag or an airtight container. It makes blending so much easier later!*

LICUADO VERDE DE PIÑA COLADA

Green Piña Colada Smoothie

I started making smoothies when my kids were young, and we were always in a hurry to get out of the house for school. At first, they obviously didn't want to drink anything green or weird-colored. However, with some practice and tips I discovered, I learned that if we gave the smoothies fun and exciting names, they would drink them. Sometimes, I even let them choose the ingredients to see which color the smoothie would turn out. That's when we began experimenting, and I felt so happy because every smoothie was nutritionally packed, which made me confident sending them off for a long day at school. This recipe came from one of those days when we had fun and experimented with smoothie recipes. We call this one a green piña colada, as it reminded us of our vacations on the beach.

SERVES 2

¼ cup sliced frozen strawberries

½ cup riced or small florets frozen cauliflower, optional

1 cup frozen pineapple

1 cup coconut milk or coconut water

½ to ¾ cup plain, unsweetened coconut yogurt or regular yogurt

1 handful spinach, about 1 cup

1 scoop vanilla plant-based or regular protein powder, optional

Place all of the ingredients in a blender. Blend until smooth and creamy, with no lumps. Serve immediately. If it is too thick, add ¼ cup more coconut milk or coconut water.

NOTES

- *Use regular coconut milk from a carton. Canned milk is too thick for this recipe.*
- *For frozen cauliflower, I usually keep cauliflower rice in my freezer, which works amazingly well in smoothies. I promise you, nobody will even taste it.*

LICUADO DE CHOCOLATE MEXICANO

Mexican Chocolate Smoothie

This breakfast smoothie has a blend of flavors inspired by a thick and rich cup of hot Mexican chocolate. I make this smoothie with raw cacao powder for its nutritional value, but unsweetened cocoa will work just as well. I also include vanilla-flavored plant-based protein to add extra fiber, vitamins, and minerals. I recommend using a good-quality protein powder without added sugars or artificial sweeteners. The combination of chocolate with vanilla, cinnamon, and cayenne pepper gives this smoothie a sweet and spicy kick at the start of your day.

SERVES 2

3 cups almond milk or other nondairy milk

2 heaping tablespoons almond butter

3 tablespoons raw cacao powder or unsweetened cocoa

¼ cup vanilla plant-based or regular protein powder

1 tablespoon ground cinnamon

⅓ to ¼ teaspoon cayenne pepper

1 handful of spinach or kale

1 or 2 dates, pitted

Place all the ingredients in a high-speed blender and blend on high speed for about 1 minute. The mixture should be smooth and creamy.

Taste the smoothie directly from the blender. If you feel it lacks sweetness, add another date. If it is too thick, add ¼ cup of plant-based milk or ½ cup of ice to thin it out. Serve immediately.

NOTE

- *For this smoothie, I use plant-based protein and almond milk, but feel free to use your favorite milk and protein powder. I recommend vanilla flavor, but chocolate will also be delicious.*

JUGO DE NARANJA Y ZARZAMORA

Blackberry-Orange Juice

My aunt and uncle had a gorgeous property in Valle de Bravo for years. Growing up, they would often invite our family to spend the weekend with them and their kids. Even my own children got to enjoy that beautiful place.

They still remember the last time we were there. They woke up early, excited, and we went blackberry picking together. Later that morning, they proudly brought their blackberries to the kitchen and made this juice—fresh, vibrant, and so full of flavor. It's one of those memories that stays with you, and now, every time I make this juice, it brings me right back to that peaceful morning in Valle de Bravo.

SERVES 4

4 to 6 fresh oranges to make 5 to 6 cups of juice or 5 cups of store-bought orange juice

1 cup fresh or frozen blackberries

Roll the oranges on the counter to loosen the juice.

Cut them in half and squeeze the juice using a citrus juicer and pour into a pitcher. Blend 1 cup of the juice with the blackberries in a blender, strain, and return to the pitcher.

Mix and serve with ice or as is.

NOTE

- *You could also serve this as agua fresca if you add sugar to taste and more water.*

AVENA PARA EL DÍA SIGUIENTE CON JARABE DE CAFÉ DE OLLA

Café de Olla Overnight Oats

I wish I had grown up waking up to the smell of café de olla, coffee simmering with cinnamon and piloncillo, but no, not even close. So now I get to re-create that dreamy combo in these overnight oats. They're quick, cozy, and perfect for mornings when you're running out the door but still want a little sabor Mexicano in your day.

SERVES 1

½ cup old-fashioned oats

½ cup plant-based milk (almond, oat, or cashew)

1 or 2 espresso shots

2 to 3 tablespoons Café de Olla Syrup (page 39)

2 tablespoons yogurt of choice, optional

1 tablespoon chia seeds

Pinch of cinnamon, optional

Pinch of kosher salt

Toppings

Orange zest

Chopped nuts (pecans or walnuts)

More Café de Olla Syrup to drizzle

In a jar or bowl, combine the oats, plant-based milk, espresso, café de olla syrup, yogurt (if using), chia seeds, cinnamon, and salt.

Mix well, cover, and refrigerate overnight (or at least 4 hours).

The next morning, give it a good stir, and top with orange zest, nuts, and an extra drizzle of café de olla syrup if needed.

Enjoy cold, or warm it slightly if you prefer.

ENSALADA DE FRUTAS

Mexican Chopped Fruit Salad

Funny story . . . growing up, I *hated* soup.

And yet, every single day after school, there it was, waiting for me at the table. A bowl of soup, steaming hot and ready to eat.

In Mexico, our main meal is 2 to 3 p.m., right after school. This was our family mealtime, a tradition we upheld every day. And the first course? Always soup. Like clockwork.

But then, there were those special days, especially in the summer, when we'd skip the soup and have a fruit salad instead. The contrast was like a breath of fresh air. Those were my favorite days. No offense to soup, but give me mango, papaya, and fresh watermelon over caldo any day.

SERVES 4

1 red or green apple, diced

1 cup diced pineapple

1 cup diced cantaloupe

1 mango, peeled and diced

1 cup diced red or yellow watermelon

1 pear, diced

Freshly squeezed juice of ½ to 1 orange

In a large bowl, combine the apple, pineapple, cantaloupe, mango, watermelon, and pear. Pour the orange juice over the fruit. Gently toss until all the fruit is coated and slightly sweetened by the juice.

Serve immediately or chill for 15 to 20 minutes before serving for an extra refreshing touch.

NOTES

- *This is the perfect clean-your-refrigerator salad; you can add all the fruit you want or any ripe fruit. If you serve it for breakfast, chill the salad for at least 10 minutes before serving. This salad is perfect for pool parties, lunch, or a healthy snack. You can add any fruit you want, but make sure you don't add bananas; they don't mix well with the rest of the fruit, and if you have leftovers, they go bad pretty fast.*
- *Serve as breakfast with a big dollop of yogurt and several tablespoons of Granola Alegría (page 79).*

MIGUITAS CON HUEVO

Mexican Migas

These are Mexican migas, very different from the Tex-Mex version (which I also love, by the way). But let's be clear: This version is the authentic Mexican thing. We don't turn them into tacos, we don't add cheese or tomatoes, and we don't add cilantro. And the base? Always corn tortillas.

Both versions are delicious, but I'm convinced nothing beats this recipe. It's one of those rare dishes I can make for my whole family, no matter what diet everyone's following. Plus, it tastes like home for me and the kids.

SERVES 2

3 corn tortillas (homemade, page 40, or store-bought), 1½ tortillas per egg

2 eggs, or ½ cup Just Egg (liquid vegan egg), or ½ cup pressed and crumbled firm tofu

2 tablespoons vegetable oil

2 tablespoons diced onion

½ teaspoon kosher salt

Salsa of choice, for serving

Cut the corn tortillas into small squares or strips. If you're using eggs, crack and whisk them in a bowl and set aside. If using liquid vegan egg, measure and set aside. If you're using tofu, press and crumble it into small pieces and set aside.

In a nonstick skillet, heat the vegetable oil over medium heat. Add the tortilla pieces and cook until they begin to turn golden and almost crispy, 3 to 5 minutes. Stir in the diced onion and add salt.

If you're using tofu, add it at this stage as well and let it brown slightly on the edges. Let everything cook together until the onion softens and the mixture becomes fragrant.

If you're using eggs or liquid Just Egg, pour them over the tortilla mixture once the onions are translucent and beginning to brown. Stir gently and cook for 1 to 2 minutes, just until the eggs are set but still soft. Serve warm with your favorite salsa.

NOTES

- *This recipe scales beautifully—just use about 1½ tortillas, 1 tablespoon diced onion, and 1 tablespoon of oil per egg. Make as many eggs as you want, and the results will always be perfect!*
- *For a larger meal, serve with refried beans or avocado on the side.*

QUESADILLAS FRITAS

Fried Quesadillas

This is probably not the best place to share this confession (sorry, Mom and Dad), but when I lived in Mexico City, my friends and I (sometimes with boyfriends in tow) would celebrate the end of final exams by driving up to El Ajusco, a national park just outside the city. Why? Because that's where you'll find some of the best fried quesadillas. Were we supposed to be driving up there as teenagers? Probably not. Oops. But the quesadillas were worth the risk of getting caught.

Crispy on the outside, soft and cheesy on the inside—these quesadillas are made with homemade masa and cheese filling. A beloved Mexican street food, they're perfect for weekend cooking or when you're craving something comforting and satisfying.

MAKES 16 QUESADILLAS

3 cups masa harina

1 teaspoon kosher salt

3 cups warm water

2½ cups grated mozzarella cheese or any other melty cheese (you can use vegan shredded mozzarella for this recipe)

1 quart vegetable oil, for frying

For serving

Salsa Verde (page 20), Salsa Verde Cruda (page 23), or your favorite salsa

Optional toppings: shredded cabbage, Guacamole (page 32), crema, or Crema de Cashews (page 34)

Cut 2 (9-inch) circles or squares from a thin plastic bag or a ziplock bag and set aside. In a pinch, you can use parchment paper. In a large bowl, combine the masa harina and salt. Gradually add the warm water, mixing with your hands until a smooth, pliable dough forms. It shouldn't be too dry or sticky. Cover with a clean kitchen towel and let rest for at least 10 minutes or up to 30 minutes.

Divide the dough into 16 equal balls, roughly the size of a golf ball. Place one piece of the prepared plastic circles on a tortilla press (see page 60). Place the masa ball in the center and cover with the other piece of plastic and press. Open the tortilla press, remove the top plastic from the tortilla, and add about 3 tablespoons of cheese to the center of the tortilla. Using the remaining plastic to assist, fold the tortilla over until all sides touch, forming a half-circle, and gently press the edges to seal.

Set a baking sheet lined with paper towels next to the stove. Heat the oil in a heavy-bottom 12-inch skillet over medium heat, aiming for a temperature of 350°F (175°C).

Fry the quesadillas in batches for 3 to 4 minutes per side, or until golden brown and crispy. Do not overcrowd the skillet; this helps maintain the oil temperature and ensures even frying. Use kitchen tongs or two fish turners to carefully flip the quesadillas and remove them from the oil. Set on the baking sheet lined with paper towels and lightly pat to remove excess oil before serving.

Serve immediately, topped with your favorite salsa, and optional garnishes like guacamole or shredded cabbage for crunch.

Continued >>

NOTES

- *You can also fill the quesadillas with cooked potatoes or a mix of potatoes and cheese. Cook 2 medium potatoes, russet or Yukon Gold, in salted water until they can be pierced with a fork without resistance. Let them cool, then peel, and mash them to the desired texture. I like my filling a bit chunky.*
- *Leftover fillings, such as Picadillo (page 128), Tinga (page 132), or Cortadillo (page 131), also work beautifully. Make sure the filling is not too saucy.*
- *Extra masa? Refrigerate or freeze it. Thaw in the refrigerator overnight and bring to room temperature before using.*
- *Clean as you go! Frying gets messy, and dried masa is much harder to clean than fresh masa.*

ENTOMATADAS DE QUESO

Corn Tortillas Smothered in Tomato Sauce

Entomatadas—and enfrijoladas, those tortillas drenched in silky, loose refried beans—are so close to my heart. When I was around ten, we had a nanny named Lupe who made the best entomatadas and enfrijoladas I've ever tasted.

The best part? She always surprised my siblings and me with them *exactly* when we needed them most. Just as we started getting hangry and picking fights, we'd catch the smell of oil and corn tortillas in the air and suddenly, peace. Lupe would walk out of the kitchen with a plate of entomatadas for each of us, and just like that, the chaos melted away.

She called me *mi niña* and my siblings *mis niños*. She loved us fiercely.

And she also loved lucha libre. But if I had to guess, I think deep down, she loved us just a little more than all her luchadores.

SERVES 4

For the sauce

2 chiles de árbol

4 medium ripe red tomatoes

¼ medium white onion

3 unpeeled garlic cloves

1 teaspoon kosher salt

2 tablespoons vegetable oil

For the entomatadas

½ medium white onion, thinly sliced or diced

2 cups of crumbled queso fresco, prepared Tofu Queso Fresco (page 36), ricotta salata, or cotija cheese

Kosher salt

8 to 12 corn tortillas (homemade, page 40, or store-bought)

Vegetable oil

For serving

Mexican crema or Crema de Cashews (page 34), optional

Fresh chopped cilantro, optional, for garnish

Thinly sliced serrano, optional, for garnish

To make the sauce

Remove the stems from the chiles de árbol. Heat a skillet over medium heat and roast the chiles until they turn darker in color, 2 to 3 minutes. Keep an eye on them and move them around so they don't burn. Remove from the skillet and set aside.

In the same skillet, roast the tomatoes, onion, and unpeeled garlic over medium heat until charred on all sides. Once ready, peel the garlic and transfer the roasted tomatoes, onion, garlic, and the roasted chiles to a blender. Add salt and blend until smooth.

In the same skillet, heat the vegetable oil. Pour in the blended sauce and simmer for a few minutes, stirring occasionally, until the flavors have deepened, the color has turned a rich, dark red, and the sauce has reduced slightly.

Continued >>

To make the entomatadas

Meanwhile, in a separate bowl, mix the sliced onion with the crumbled queso fresco. Taste and add a pinch of salt if needed. Set aside.

Next, lightly fry the tortillas in a small amount of oil—just enough to make them soft and pliable without becoming crispy.

To serve

Assemble just before serving. Dip each tortilla into the warm tomato sauce, then place it on a plate. Fill the tortilla with the queso fresco mix, then fold or roll it. Repeat with the remaining tortillas, serving them on a platter or individual plates with the crema, cilantro, and serrano slices, if using.

NOTES

- *Lightly fry the tortillas until just pliable; if they are too oily the sauce won't stick.*
- *Very thin tortillas tend to break, especially once dipped in sauce. Look for corn tortillas that are a bit thicker and sturdier.*
- *Warm tortillas are easier to work with. Cold tortillas crack more easily when folded or filled.*
- *The tomato sauce should be warm, not boiling. If it's too hot, it can soften the tortillas too much and cause tearing.*
- *Don't soak the tortillas in the sauce—a quick dip is enough.*

ENMOLADAS DE NADA

Mole-Drenched Tortillas

Mole isn't just a sauce, it's the Sauce. It's bold. It's complex. It's Mexico on a plate.

Whether it's mole poblano or mole oaxaqueño, this isn't something you drizzle and forget—it's a full-on celebration of flavor, tradition, and identity.

Too often, mole gets dismissed as just a "chocolaty sauce." Let's set the record straight: Mole is magic. Sweet, spicy, earthy, nutty, it's all in there, layered and perfectly balanced. Every version tells a story, and every family has their own.

Serve it solo (trust me, it can hold its own), or pour it over enchiladas stuffed with cheese, shredded chicken, or even Tofu Queso Fresco (page 36). However you serve it, mole doesn't play the background. It is the moment.

For this recipe, I use store-bought mole—but don't skimp. Go for the good stuff: I love the Oaxacan-style mole from La Guelaguetza (ilovemole.com) or the Hernán brand for a classic poblano version.

SERVES 4

2 cups mole (made according to package instructions)

Kosher salt, if needed

4 tablespoons neutral oil

8 corn tortillas (homemade, page 40, or store-bought)

Toppings

Thinly sliced red onion

Sliced avocado

Sesame seeds

Crema de Cashews (page 34) or crema

Crumbled cotija cheese (use crumbled feta for a plant-based option)

In a saucepan over medium heat, warm the mole, adding salt to taste, if needed.

Heat the oil in a skillet and lightly fry each tortilla for 10 to 15 seconds per side—just enough to soften them without making them crispy. Set them aside on a plate lined with paper towels.

Using kitchen tongs, dip each tortilla into the warm mole sauce until fully coated. Fold in half or into quarters and place on a serving plate or individual plates.

Once all the tortillas are coated and arranged, drizzle with extra mole and top with your favorite garnishes like onion, avocado, sesame seeds, crema, or cotija cheese.

NOTES

- *These enmoladas are filling-free, but you can always add sautéed vegetables, beans, shredded chicken, pork, scrambled eggs, or cheese if you'd like.*
- *Mole flavors can vary depending on the type used (mole poblano, mole negro oaxaqueño, etc.), so adjust the seasoning to your taste. Always read the package instructions on how to prepare the mole; they may specify to add chocolate or roasted tomatoes based on the region of the mole.*
- *Make it a full meal by serving it with a side of Arroz Blanco (page 35) and Frijolitos Refritos (page 37). Homemade corn tortillas work exceptionally well with this dish and the Entomatadas de Queso (page 61). Store-bought tortillas that are thicker work best for this recipe.*
- *Quick tip: You can also make chilaquiles with the mole sauce.*
- *See the Entomatadas de Queso notes (page 63), as they apply here as well.*

CHILAQUILES CON SALSA DE TRES CHILES

Three Chiles Chilaquiles

When it comes to making chilaquiles, you can make them "the authentic way or the lazy way," as my grandma would say. The traditional method involves frying tortilla pieces, which can be time-consuming and messy. Instead, I use thick store-bought corn tortilla chips, which make this dish quick and convenient, whether I'm making a late-night snack after a party or breakfast. And the best part? They will be bursting with flavor!

SERVES 6

For the three chiles sauce

1 medium guajillo chile

1 medium ancho chile

1 medium pasilla chile

6 medium tomatoes, about 1½ pounds

½ large yellow onion, roughly chopped

4 unpeeled garlic cloves

1¼ cups vegetable broth or water

1 tablespoon kosher salt

2 tablespoons vegetable oil

For the chilaquiles

12 ounces homemade tortilla chips (page 43) or 1 (12-ounce) bag thick corn chips

¼ cup thinly sliced red onion

2 tablespoons chopped cilantro

¼ cup crema

1 avocado, sliced, optional

To make the three chiles sauce

Heat a 12-inch skillet over medium-high heat. Add the chiles, whole tomatoes, onion, and garlic to the dry skillet. Roast the chiles for 2 to 3 minutes, then remove from the heat and set aside. Continue roasting the rest of the vegetables, turning them regularly, until you see charred patches on all sides and the tomato skins start to peel. This should take about 8 minutes.

Once done, remove the garlic skins, chile stems, and chile seeds, and place with the rest of the vegetables in a blender with the vegetable broth and salt. Blend the sauce until smooth.

Next, heat the vegetable oil in the same skillet, and pour in the sauce. Cook the sauce while stirring occasionally, 5 to 8 minutes.

To make the chilaquiles

Add the tortilla chips into the skillet and carefully coat them with the sauce or serve the tortilla chips in a bowl and pour the sauce directly into them. Serve immediately while the chips are still crunchy. Finish with the red onion, cilantro, crema, and avocado (if using).

NOTES

- **CLASSIC CHILAQUILES WITH FRIED EGG:** *Top the chilaquiles with a fried egg, sunny-side up. The runny yolk adds a creamy texture that beautifully complements the crunch of the tortilla chips.*
- **CHILAQUILES WITH CREMA AND CHEESE:** *Drizzle some crema over the chilaquiles and sprinkle a generous amount of crumbled queso fresco or cotija cheese on top. This combination provides a rich, tangy flavor that balances the spicy chile sauce.*
- **CHILAQUILES WITH VEGAN CREMA AND CHEESE:** *Drizzle Crema de Cashews (page 34) and serve with vegan feta cheese or prepared Tofu Queso Fresco (page 36). The vegan feta cheese brand that I like for this dish is Follow Your Heart.*
- **SIMPLE CHILAQUILES:** *For a dairy-free version, serve the chilaquiles plain or topped with diced onions, sliced avocado, and fresh cilantro. This version lets the flavor of the chile sauce shine through.*

CHILAQUILES CON SALSA DE FRIJOLES MANEADOS

Chilaquiles with Maneado Bean Sauce

I love frijoles maneados. They're not your typical refried beans. They're from northern Mexico and they are rich, smoky, a little spicy, and have the smoothest, almost silky texture. When I was developing this recipe and decided to serve it as chilaquiles, I truly thought I was innovating, like starting a whole new bean revolution.

Then I shared it with my mom—who's from Sinaloa—and she just smiled and said, "Sí, están deliciosos. Deberías probarlos con tortillas fritas, quedan buenísimos." (Yes, they're delicious. You should try them with fried tortillas—they're so good.)

So, no big innovation here. Turns out, this dish was already stored in my DNA.

SERVES 4

For the bean-chile sauce

2 dried guajillo chiles, stemmed and seeded

2 cups boiling water, for soaking

1 chipotle chile in adobo sauce (use 2 for more heat)

3 garlic cloves

¼ small white onion

¼ teaspoon ground cumin

1 tablespoon kosher salt

2 (15-ounce) cans pinto beans, drained

1 tablespoon olive oil

1 tablespoon butter, optional (for richness)

1 cup shredded cheese (queso Oaxaca, Monterey Jack, mozzarella, or vegan cheese)

For serving

12 ounces thick tortilla chips (homemade, page 43, or store-bought)

Mexican crema or vegan crema

Crumbled cotija cheese, queso fresco, feta, or vegan alternative such as prepared Tofu Queso Fresco (page 36) or vegan feta

Chopped cilantro

Thinly sliced onion

To make the bean-chile sauce

Soak the guajillo chiles in boiling water for 10 to 15 minutes, until soft and pliable.

Blend the softened chiles with their soaking water, the chipotle, garlic, onion, cumin, salt, and pinto beans until smooth.

Heat the olive oil and butter (if using) in a large skillet over medium heat. Pour in the bean sauce and simmer for about 5 minutes, until heated through and bubbling.

Turn off the heat and stir in the shredded cheese. The sauce should be pourable. Add a splash of water if needed to loosen it up.

To serve

Place the crispy tortilla chips in a large bowl. Pour the warm bean sauce over the chips and toss gently to coat.

Top with crema, crumbled cheese, fresh cilantro, and thinly sliced onion. Serve hot.

NOTES

- *Short on time? Skip the dried chiles and use a 3-ounce can of chipotle chiles in adobo instead. Blend directly with the beans and continue as directed.*
- *Make it a full meal: Add a fried egg on top or serve alongside grilled meats, grilled tofu, or roasted vegetables.*

TOSTADAS DE HUEVO EN SALSA DE AJONJOLÍ

Egg Tostadas with Chile-Sesame Sauce

Creamy, nutty, and a little spicy, this rich sesame-chile sauce brings a bold and delicious twist to your breakfast tostadas. Top with saucy scrambled eggs or tofu, refried beans, and thinly sliced red onion for a savory and satisfying brunch or dinner dish. My hope is that once you try this salsa, your imagination explodes—you'll want to pour it over everything. It's that good.

SERVES 4 TO 6

For the chile-sesame sauce

3 dried chiles de árbol (adjust to taste)

3 dried guajillo chiles

3 unpeeled garlic cloves

3 medium tomatoes

¼ small white onion, roughly chopped

½ cup unroasted sesame seeds

2 cups water (plus more if needed)

¼ teaspoon freshly ground black pepper

Pinch of ground cloves

2 tablespoons kosher salt (or to taste)

1 tablespoon vegetable oil

For the eggs

Neutral oil, for sautéing

½ cup sliced white onion

4 to 6 eggs, or 1 cup Just Egg, or 1 cup crumbled tofu

2 teaspoons kosher salt

For the tostadas

6 tostadas

1½ cups Frijolitos Refritos (page 37)

Thinly sliced red onion, for garnish

Cilantro, for garnish

To make the sauce

Heat a dry skillet over medium heat. Toast the chiles de árbol, guajillo chiles, and unpeeled garlic cloves for 2 to 3 minutes, until the chiles puff slightly and darken and the garlic turns golden. Be careful not to burn them. Remove the stems and seeds from the chiles, peel the garlic, and transfer to a blender.

In the same skillet, char the tomatoes and onion until blackened in spots. Turn off the heat and add them to the blender with the chiles and garlic.

Toast the sesame seeds in the still-warm skillet, stirring constantly until golden and fragrant, 2 to 3 minutes. Add to the blender.

Add the water, black pepper, ground cloves, and salt to taste (start with 1 tablespoon if you're unsure). Blend until completely smooth, adding more water if needed for a thick but pourable consistency.

Heat the oil in a deep skillet or saucepan over medium-low heat (to avoid splatters).

Pour in the blended sauce and simmer for 5 to 7 minutes, stirring often to prevent sticking or splattering. You may partially cover the pan with a lid.

Continued >>

To prepare the eggs

Heat about 1 teaspoon of oil in a nonstick skillet over medium heat. Sauté the sliced onion until soft and translucent.

Add the eggs, Just Egg, or crumbled tofu. Season with salt and scramble gently until just set.

Pour in about 1 cup of the chili sesame sauce and stir to coat. Remove from heat.

To assemble the tostadas

Spread each tostada with a generous layer of frijolitos refritos. Top with a spoonful or two of the saucy scrambled eggs. Finish with sliced red onion and cilantro and serve immediately.

NOTES

- *Use up the salsa: This sauce is magic. Use leftovers for enchiladas—dip warm corn tortillas in the sauce, fill with sautéed vegetables or shredded chicken, and roll.*
- *Try it with chicken: Pan fry chicken pieces, pour the sauce over, cover, and simmer until cooked through.*
- *Make ahead: The sauce keeps well in the refrigerator for up to 5 days and can be frozen for later.*
- *Salt note: The full batch calls for 2 tablespoons kosher salt, but if you're sensitive to salt or plan to use the sauce later (like in enchiladas), start with 1 tablespoon and adjust to taste after blending.*
- *Sauce-to-egg ratio: For saucy eggs, 4 eggs plus 1 cup sauce is great. For less saucy eggs, go with 6 eggs or reduce the amount of sauce.*

COFFEE CAKE CON HARINA DE MAÍZ

Masa Coffee Cake

The idea for this coffee cake came from tamales dulces. It wasn't until I moved to the United States that I learned about tamaladas—those gatherings where everyone makes tamales together. I didn't grow up making tamales with my grandmothers, but my paternal grandmother always had tamales at home, usually from a place in Mexico City called La Flor de Lis.

My favorites were the ones wrapped in banana leaves, filled with salsa verde—savory, comforting, everything I loved. But she also always had tamales dulces—those soft, pink ones with raisins, meant for the kids. I never quite understood the raisins, but I remember them vividly.

This coffee cake takes me right back to her house. It's sweet, made with masa harina and cinnamon, like those tamales dulces she always bought for us. I wasn't the biggest fan of the pink tamales back then (I've always leaned savory), but something about this cake feels like a hug from her kitchen.

SERVES 9 TO 12

For the streusel topping

¾ cup all-purpose flour

½ cup granulated sugar

1 tablespoon ground cinnamon

1 teaspoon ground chile ancho

½ cup chopped pecans or walnuts

⅓ cup melted butter or vegan butter

For the cake

1 cup unsweetened plant milk (soy, almond, or oat works well)

1 tablespoon apple cider vinegar or lemon juice

½ cup masa harina (yellow masa harina has more flavor)

1¼ cups all-purpose flour

½ cup granulated sugar

1 tablespoon baking powder

1 teaspoon salt

¼ cup sour cream or vegan sour cream

⅓ cup vegetable oil or melted vegan butter

Preheat the oven to 350°F and grease an 8-inch baking pan.

Make the streusel topping by whisking together the flour, sugar, cinnamon, and ground chile ancho in a medium bowl until well combined. Stir in the chopped nuts. Pour the melted butter over the dry mixture. Use a fork or your hands to mix until crumbly and evenly moistened. The texture should resemble coarse crumbs. Set aside until ready to use.

To make the cake, in a small bowl, combine the plant milk with the vinegar, stir, and set aside.

In a medium bowl, whisk together the masa harina, flour, sugar, baking powder, and salt.

Whisk the sour cream until creamy in a large bowl and add the oil. Mix until everything is well integrated.

Continued >>

Add half of the dry ingredients to the sour cream mixture and mix. Add the milk with vinegar; stir until just combined, being careful not to overmix. Add the rest of the dry ingredients and continue mixing.

Pour the batter into the prepared baking pan. Sprinkle the topping generously over the cake before baking.

Bake for 20 to 25 minutes at, or until the edges are golden brown and a toothpick inserted into the center of the coffee cake comes out clean or with a few crumbs.

Let the coffee cake cool before serving.

NOTES

- *Ground chile ancho is easy to find in the spice section of most supermarkets, but if you cannot find it, it is simple to make at home. Remove the stems and seeds from dried ancho chiles, lightly toast them in a dry skillet until fragrant, let cool completely, then grind to a very fine powder and sift. Store in an airtight jar away from heat and light.*

CONCHAS DE MAZAPÁN

Mazapán-Topped Conchas

Once, while visiting family in Mexico City, my husband and I decided to wake up early and wander around the city, no plan, just the two of us and the quiet streets. We were walking until the smell of fresh-baked bread stopped us in our tracks. We followed the scent and ended up at the tiniest, most charming bakery that, to our surprise, specialized in only conchas.

Big conchas, tiny conchas, even savory ones (which was completely new to us). We ordered coffee and grabbed a couple of the conchas that had just come out of the oven, *conchas de mazapán*. They were hot, buttery, and absolutely perfect.

With the first bite, we both froze, covered in concha crust, and looked at each other, and he said, "Please make this at home."

MAKES 12 TO 16 CONCHAS

For the conchas

1 packet (7g) instant fast-rise dry yeast

1 cup warm water, 105°F to 115°F (40 to 46°C)

½ cup and 1 tablespoon granulated sugar, divided

4 cups all-purpose flour

1 teaspoon kosher salt

½ cup plain Greek yogurt or unsweetened plant-based yogurt

1 stick (½ cup) unsalted butter, at room temperature

For the topping (concha crust)

¾ cup unsalted butter, at room temperature, about 170 grams

½ cup smooth peanut butter, salted or unsalted

Pinch of kosher salt

1½ cups all-purpose flour

1¼ cups powdered sugar

To make the conchas, in a small bowl, dissolve the yeast in the warm water with 1 tablespoon of sugar. Let it sit for 10 minutes, or until it becomes foamy. In the bowl of a stand mixer fitted with the hook attachment, mix the flour, remaining ½ cup sugar, and salt. Add the yogurt and foamy yeast mixture.

Gradually add the butter and knead for 10 to 15 minutes, until the dough is smooth and elastic. It should not stick to the bowl. The dough might look rough or messy at first; don't worry, it comes together.

Cover and let it rise in a warm place until double in size, about 1 hour. If you want to shorten the rising time, place the dough in the bowl of an Instant Pot, cover with plastic, and set it to the yogurt function. If you use the Instant Pot method to proof the dough, let it get to room temperature before handling.

Remove the dough from the bowl and knead it for a minute on a lightly floured surface. Using your floured hands, divide the dough into 10 to 12 equal balls, conchas, each weighing about 110 grams.

Continued >>

Place them on a baking sheet lined with parchment paper, cover with plastic wrap, and begin preparing the topping.

Prepare the peanut butter topping by beating the butter until creamy, then add the peanut butter and salt and mix well. Add the flour and powdered sugar and continue mixing until a dough forms. The dough should be soft and resemble Play-Doh.

Divide this dough based on the number of conchas you have, rolling each portion into a ball and flattening it with a rolling pin or a tortilla press (see page 60) lined with either plastic wrap or parchment paper. Apply the topping to each concha individually, ensuring it is larger than the concha itself.

Let the shaped conchas rise again for about 30 minutes, until puffy.

Preheat the oven to 180°C (350°F).

Bake the conchas for 18 to 20 minutes, or until lightly golden on top. Enjoy warm.

NOTES

- *Make sure the oven rack is in the middle of the oven, because the topping can brown really fast. Do not overcrowd the baking sheets; four conchas per half sheet is good. You can also make smaller conchas.*
- *Vegan butter brands vary in fat and water content, which can affect spread, browning, and texture. For best baking results, choose a high-fat, stick-style vegan butter with a clean flavor (Miyoko's or Flora work beautifully). Avoid tub-style spreads, as they contain more water and may change the final texture.*

GRANOLA ALEGRÍA

Popped Amaranth Granola

Amaranth, a pre-Hispanic grain, is one of the most nutritious foods from civilizations like the Aztecs and Mayans. When I was growing up in the 1980s, Corn Pops and other all-American cereals were a hit back in Mexico City. I remember being obsessed with Corn Pops. My mom, who has never been a huge fan of processed food, let us eat store-bought sugary cereal only if we added a large spoonful of puffed amaranth.

I must confess that I did the same for my kids until I discovered that you could cook and make things with it. This is one of my favorite ways to use this amazingly delicious grain. It is inspired by traditional Mexican sweets called alegrías, which are made primarily from puffed amaranth seeds and sweeteners like honey or piloncillo. The name Alegría means *joy*, and a granola named alegría is a glorious way to start the day.

MAKES ABOUT 6 CUPS

2 cups rolled oats

1 cup popped amaranth (or raw if you want it crunchier after baking)

1 cup chopped nuts (almonds, walnuts, or pecans)

½ cup pumpkin seeds (pepitas) or sunflower seeds

½ cup shredded coconut

1 tablespoon cinnamon

Pinch of kosher salt

⅔ cup maple syrup or honey

⅓ cup vegetable oil or coconut oil

½ cup dried fruit (cranberries, raisins, or chopped dates)

Preheat the oven to 325°F (165°C) and line a baking sheet with parchment paper.

In a large bowl, combine the oats, popped amaranth, nuts, pumpkin seeds, coconut, cinnamon, and salt.

In a small bowl, whisk the maple syrup and oil together. Pour the wet mixture into the dry ingredients and stir well until evenly coated.

Spread the granola on the baking sheet in an even layer. Bake for 20 to 25 minutes, stirring halfway, until golden and fragrant. Please don't leave the granola unchecked, as it will burn easily.

Let cool completely, then add the dried fruit.

Store in an airtight container for up to 3 weeks.

NOTES

- *Do yourself a favor and measure the oil first in a measuring cup; then measure the maple syrup in the same cup and it will glide off.*
- *You can find popped amaranth in any health store or order it online.*

GARIBALDIS

Apricot-Glazed Upside-Down Pound Cake Muffins

In Mexico City, there's a bakery called El Globo. When I was growing up, it was the place we went to buy pan dulce. This was many years ago, when it was still a small chain—elegant yet approachable—and known for crafting the best pan dulce in a slightly more refined manner than the classic neighborhood panaderías.

One of the things I remember most was their mini versions of all the classic favorites: Orejas (page 174) and Garibaldis. They'd carefully place the little pieces of bread on a white tray, wrap it in thin white paper, and then tie them with cotton twine. I remember exactly how they tied it—because on the ride home, my siblings and I would always try to sneak a piece, but it was impossible to open without getting caught.

Garibaldis are small, golden, buttery sponge cakes brushed with apricot glaze and completely coated in white nonpareil sprinkles. Sweet, sticky, and with the perfect little crunch from the sprinkles—they're irresistible. I still dream about them.

MAKES 24

2 cups all-purpose flour

1½ teaspoons baking powder

½ teaspoon baking soda

½ teaspoon kosher salt

1 cup butter (2 sticks), room temperature (vegan butter or vegetable oil if you want them vegan)

1½ cups granulated sugar

¾ cup unflavored and unsweetened Greek regular or vegan yogurt

2 teaspoons vanilla extract

½ cup almond milk, oat milk, or dairy milk

For the topping

1 cup apricot jam

2 tablespoons lemon juice

1 cup white mini nonpareils

Preheat the oven to 350°F and line 24 muffin cups with parchment liners.

In a large bowl, mix the flour, baking powder, baking soda, and salt until thoroughly combined. In the bowl of a stand mixer fitted with the paddle attachment, cream the butter and sugar. Add the yogurt, vanilla, and milk.

Slowly add the flour mixture, being careful not to overmix. When everything is well combined, divide the batter into the muffin pans. Avoid overfilling each muffin cup, aiming for a flat top when they come out of the oven. Bake for 20 minutes, then cool on a wire rack.

While the muffins cool, make the topping. Mix the apricot jam with the lemon juice and set aside. Carefully remove the liners from the muffins, flipping them so the tops are on the rack. Place the nonpareils in a bowl and set aside.

To coat the garibaldis, take one muffin and carefully brush all the sides and the top (formerly the bottom) with the apricot-lemon mixture. Holding the brushed muffin over the nonpareils' bowl, spoon them over until it is completely covered. Repeat this process for all the muffins.

You can freeze half of the muffin batch without coating them in jam and nonpareils, then thaw and finish when ready to eat.

BOTANAS

STARTERS

Botanas are more than just Mexican appetizers—they're an excuse to gather, to pause the day, and to enjoy the moment. You'll find them at parties, of course, but also when watching a soccer game, playing a board game with your kids, or simply catching up with a friend. They can be as simple as potato chips, some marinated olives, or tortilla chips with guacamole, or as thoughtful as homemade tortitas de papa or queso en salsa—but what they all have in common is that they bring people together.

When I moved to the United States, I realized how much I missed that casual magic of "una botanita y un vinito." Back home, it didn't need to be a full meal, a big occasion, or a planned invitation. Someone would say, "¿Vienes por una botanita?" or if someone showed up at your door, you just let them in and hook them up with a good agua fresca or a cold beer, and you just knew you were in for good conversation, lots of laughs, and probably enough food to skip dinner.

For me, that's still the perfect plan. No pressure, no fuss—just something to nibble on, something to sip, and the people you love around you. Some days it's chips and a beautiful cheeseboard with salsa macha on the side; other days, when I have a bit more time, I'll make something warm and nostalgic, like those crispy gorditas my kids love.

That's the thing about botanas. They're not just starters—they're the start of something good.

AGUACHILE NEGRO DE NOPALES Y PALMITO

Black Aguachile with Nopales and Hearts of Palm

What is aguachile?

Aguachile is such a fantastic Mexican dish that's fresh, vibrant, and bursting with bold flavors! Originated from Sinaloa, the most known version features raw shrimp that get "cooked" in tangy lime juice and blended chiles. But the truth is you can make it with anything. It's amazing how aguachile has grown into a super versatile and customizable dish over the years! Think of it as ceviche's spicier cousin, often mixed with zesty fresh chiles, lime juice, and a generous sprinkle of salt. You really can't go wrong with this tasty treat!

You can get creative with the base—using shrimp, grilled meat, fruits, vegetables, mushrooms, hearts of palm, or even tofu. This Aguachile Negro version gets its name from the dark, savory sauce made with soy, Maggi sauce, and Worcestershire sauce, balanced by the heat of jalapeños and the citrusy flavor of lime. It's fresh, bold, and 100 percent plant-based if you use vegan Worcestershire sauce. Serve it in a large bowl or molcajete with tostadas on the side, and let everyone dig in.

SERVES 4 TO 6

¼ cup fresh lime juice

1 small garlic clove, grated

2 teaspoons Maggi seasoning sauce

¼ cup soy sauce

1 teaspoon regular or vegan Worcestershire sauce

1 jalapeño, thinly sliced (keep seeds for more heat)

2 teaspoons kosher salt

1 (30-ounce) jar nopales, drained and cut into bite-size pieces

1 (14-ounce) can hearts of palm (palmitos), sliced

¼ cup thinly sliced into slivers or quarter moons red onion

1 avocado, sliced or diced

¼ cup chopped fresh cilantro

Tostadas or tortilla chips (homemade, page 43, or store-bought), for serving

In a large bowl, whisk together the lime juice, grated garlic, Maggi sauce, soy sauce, Worcestershire sauce, jalapeño slices, and salt. Taste and adjust the salt—remember that soy and Maggi can vary in saltiness.

Add the nopales, hearts of palm, and red onion to the sauce. Toss gently to coat everything evenly. Let sit for at least 10 minutes so the flavors come together and the onion softens slightly. Just before serving, top with avocado slices and chopped cilantro. Serve chilled with crunchy tostadas or tortilla chips.

NOTES

- *Vegan Worcestershire sauce can be harder to find in some supermarkets, but it is widely available online and worth keeping in your pantry. The main difference is that traditional Worcestershire sauce is made with anchovies, while vegan versions replace the fish with ingredients like shiitake mushrooms or tamari to create that same deep, umami flavor. The result is slightly earthier but just as savory and complex. Omit if you can't find it.*

VERDURITAS CON CHILE

Crudités with Homemade Chile Powder

This is a true Mexican classic. When you're little, it shows up in your lunchbox. Later, it becomes your go-to snack for that afternoon hunger attack that sneaks up on you. We Mexicans love our verduritas—so much so that there are even street carts dedicated to selling them.

Growing up, this was part of every weekend at home. During botana time, there were always verduritas con chile, some kind of potato chip, and something a little more elaborate, like a tiradito or a dressed-up cheese plate. It was never fancy, but it always felt like a celebration.

SERVES 4

2 carrots, peeled and cut into sticks

1 cucumber, peeled and cut into sticks, or 4 Turkish cucumbers, quartered

1 jicama, peeled and cut into sticks

Juice of 1 lime

Tajín or Tajín Hecho en Casa (page 34)

Arrange the carrots, cucumber, and jicama on a large platter. Squeeze fresh lime juice all over, then generously sprinkle with Tajín or your favorite chilito. That's it—simple, fresh, and full of flavor.

NOTE

- *How to peel a jicama: First, rinse and dry the jicama to remove any dirt from the skin. Next, slice off both ends with a sharp knife to create a stable base. Use either a knife or a vegetable peeler to remove the thick, papery skin. While a peeler can work, using a knife is often easier since the skin is tough. Once peeled, cut the jicama into sticks, cubes, or slices as needed.*

BRIE AL HORNO CON SALSA DE MACHA Y MIEL

Baked Brie with Salsa Macha, Honey, and Dried Cherries

Sweet, spicy, creamy, and a little chewy—this baked Brie is a total flavor bomb. Whether it's a revamped '80s appetizer or a modern twist on a classic, one thing's for sure: It takes 5 minutes to prep and a lifetime to forget. Serve it with tortilla chips or melba toasts and watch it disappear.

SERVES 6 TO 8

4 tablespoons Salsa Macha (page 24) or store-bought

1 to 2 tablespoons honey

1 tablespoon chopped dried cherries or cranberries

1 (8-ounce) wheel Brie

Tortilla chips (homemade, page 43, or store-bought), melba toasts, or crusty bread

Preheat the oven to 400°F (200°C).

In a small bowl, mix the salsa macha, honey, and dried cherries. Place the Brie in a small baking dish. Spoon the salsa macha mixture over the top. Bake for 10 minutes, or until the cheese is soft and gooey in the center.

Serve warm with tortilla chips, melba toasts, or crusty bread.

NOTE

- *You should have enough macha and honey mix to cover the Brie wheel.*

NUECES PICOSAS CON TAJÍN

Spicy Nut Mix with Tajín

This is a totally guilt-free botana. These spicy nuts are made with lime juice and chile powder—no oil—and roasted until perfectly crunchy. You can snack on them all day and still feel good about it! When I lived in Mexico, I used to make tray after tray of these and give them as teacher gifts. They look beautiful packed in clear acrylic boxes with a cute ribbon—simple, delicious, and always a hit.

MAKES 2 CUPS

¼ cup aquafaba (liquid from canned chickpeas) or 1 egg white

1 tablespoon lime juice

2 cups raw almonds, pecans, cashews, or a mix

2 to 3 tablespoons Tajín

1 teaspoon kosher salt

Preheat the oven to its lowest temperature (usually 200 to 225°F / 95 to 110°C).

In a large bowl, whisk the aquafaba with the lime juice until it's foamy and light. Add the nuts and toss to coat thoroughly. Using a slotted spoon, transfer them to a baking sheet lined with parchment paper, leaving any extra liquid behind.

Sprinkle the Tajín and salt evenly over the nuts and toss gently to coat.

Spread the nuts in a single layer and bake for about 1 hour, or until dry and crisp. Stir halfway through for even roasting.

Let them cool completely before storing them.

NOTES

- *Stir or shake the nuts halfway through baking for even crispiness.*
- *If you don't have Tajín, use Tajín Hecho en Casa (page 34) or your favorite seasoned chile powder. Taste the chile powder first—if it's not salted, add a pinch of salt to balance the flavor.*
- *To make them in the air fryer, set the temperature to 300°F (149°C) and cook for 10 to 15 minutes, shaking the basket every 3 to 5 minutes.*

PAPITAS CON CHIPOTLE Y LIMÓN

Lime-Chipotle Braised Potatoes

There's something about the flavor combination of lime and chipotle that always feels just right. The moment I smell it, I already know the dish is going to be spicy, tangy, and completely irresistible. These little potatoes are slow-cooked in a bold blend of lime juice and smoky chipotle, and they always disappear fast—whether I serve them as a casual botana or as a side dish at dinner.

If you're serving them as an appetizer, I love putting them in a big bowl with bamboo skewers or toothpicks nearby. It makes it easy for everyone to snack while they sip on their first drink. Beer, tequila, or a chilled, crisp white wine all pair beautifully.

And if you have leftovers? They're just as good the next day. Smash and air fry them and then toss into a salad or serve them over a bed of homemade hummus for an easy, satisfying no-cook lunch. You can even bring them to a carne asada and serve them as part of the spread as a side dish; people will always go back for seconds.

SERVES 6 TO 8

2 chipotle peppers in adobo sauce

½ cup lime juice (about 5 limes)

½ cup olive oil

3 teaspoons kosher salt

2 pounds of the smallest potatoes you can find, washed and patted dry

1 teaspoon Mexican oregano

Finishing salt

Place the chipotle peppers, lime juice, olive oil, and kosher salt in a blender and pulse until well combined.

Place the clean potatoes in a 4-quart cast-iron braiser or 12-inch sauté pan with a lid. Pour the sauce over the potatoes, cover the pan, and cook over low heat for 30 minutes. Check the potatoes by poking them with a fork to ensure they're cooked through. Finish with the oregano and a pinch of finishing salt. Serve at room temperature.

NOTE

- *If the potatoes are not small enough, cut them in half or quarters.*
- *Because this is an oil-based sauce, natural separation will occur as it sits. This is completely normal.*

RICOTTA CON PICO DE GALLO Y ACEITUNAS VERDES

Whipped Ricotta with Pico de Gallo and Green Olives

This combo might sound a little unexpected—ricotta, feta, pico de gallo, and green olives? It's like a cultural mash-up on a plate. But trust me, it *totally* works.

It's creamy, salty, fresh, tangy—like gathering all the ingredients of my favorite dish from Veracruz and serving them as a snackable botana. It's the best part of the meal, turned into a dip you can scoop up with pita chips or veggies.

SERVES 6 TO 8

15 to 18 ounces whole-milk ricotta cheese or almond ricotta

2 to 3 tablespoons extra virgin olive oil

Zest of ½ lime

1 teaspoon kosher salt

Freshly ground black pepper

For the pico de gallo with olives

1 large tomato, diced, or 1 cup quartered cherry tomatoes

3 tablespoons finely chopped red onion

1 chile serrano or jalapeño (see notes)

Juice of 1 lime

¼ cup chopped green olives (Castelvetrano are best here)

2 tablespoons chopped fresh cilantro

Kosher salt

8 ounces feta cheese, vegan feta, or queso fresco, crumbled

Toasted pita bread, tortilla chips (homemade, page 43, or store-bought), or crusty bread for serving

Blend the ricotta with the olive oil, lime zest, salt, and black pepper in a food processor until smooth and creamy. If it's too thick, add a bit more oil or a splash of water.

To make the pico de gallo with olives, in a small bowl, combine the tomato, red onion, chile serrano, lime juice, green olives, and cilantro. Add salt to taste and let the mixture sit for a few minutes to allow the flavors to meld.

Spread the whipped ricotta in a shallow bowl or plate. Generously spoon the pico de gallo with olives over the top. Drizzle with a bit more olive oil, if desired. Finish by sprinkling the crumbled feta on top and serve with bread or chips.

NOTES

- *You can make this pico de gallo with or without chiles, but I highly recommend adding them. Jalapeños are milder, while serrano peppers bring more heat. You can slice or chop them, depending on your preference.*
- *Sometimes I slice the chiles, so their flavor infuses the pico, and they're easy to spot (and remove) for anyone who doesn't want the heat.*
- *Another option is to cut them in half, remove the seeds and veins, then finely chop—this way, you get all the flavor without too much spiciness.*
- *My favorite way of serving this is with pita chips, which may be new to some, but in Mexico, we eat a lot of pita bread; we even have tacos made with it in some taquerías.*
- *Kite Hill has a fantastic almond ricotta, and Violife makes a salty and delicious vegan feta.*

QUESO EN SALSA ROJA

Cheese in Salsa Roja

Most Mexican recipes are wonderfully multifunctional. As I mentioned in the previous chapters, if you've got a good salsa, beans, rice, and tortillas, you already have the building blocks for a full meal. This dish—call it a salsa, a dip, or a main—shows off that versatility beautifully.

Serve this in a molcajete for the full Mexican experience, and suddenly it becomes the centerpiece of your table. Scoop it up with tortilla chips, use it to fill tacos, drizzle it over rice, or serve it alongside beans and warm tortillas for a complete, satisfying meal.

SERVES 4

¼ medium white or yellow onion

3 Roma tomatoes, halved

2 garlic cloves

1 teaspoon kosher salt

2 tablespoons olive oil

3 chiles de árbol

1 (8-ounce) package Halloumi or panela, diced into 1-inch pieces

Corn tortillas (homemade, page 40, or store-bought), for serving

Tortilla chips (homemade, page 43, or store-bought), for serving

Place the onion, tomato, garlic and salt in a blender, and blend, adding a splash of water if needed.

Add the olive oil to a medium skillet over medium heat and pour in the salsa. Remove the stems of the chiles and add them to the salsa. Let the salsa cook for 5 to 8 minutes; you will see it start to change color to a bright red.

Add the diced Halloumi and serve in a bowl or a molcajete. As a dipping sauce, serve with corn tortilla chips and corn tortillas.

NOTES

- *Finish with diced red onion, chopped cilantro, and diced avocado.*
- *If you want your salsa spicier, blend the chiles with the salsa ingredients.*
- *For a vegan version, use a diced block of vegan cheese or a grillable vegan cheese, such as Violife Mediterranean-style cheese.*

TIRADITO DE HALLOUMI

Halloumi Tiradito with Citrus Sauce

Tiradito de Halloumi is my fresh, meatless take on a dish that's surprisingly common in Mexico. While tiradito has Peruvian origins, the thin slices of raw fish dressed in a citrusy, spicy sauce have been embraced in many coastal regions of Mexico and adapted with local flavors and ingredients.

In this version, I skip the fish and use cold, thinly sliced Halloumi as a substitute for queso panela; use panela if you can find a good, authentic one. It's briny, creamy, and holds up beautifully against the bright lime-chile dressing. The result is a refreshing, bold botana that's somewhere between a ceviche and a cheese plate and perfect for hot days, gatherings, or when you want something unexpected yet familiar.

SERVES 4

2 tablespoons soy sauce

2 tablespoons lime juice

2 tablespoons orange juice

1 tablespoon rice vinegar

1 tablespoon toasted sesame oil

Pinch of kosher salt

¼ cup finely sliced red onion

1 (8-ounce) pack of Halloumi or queso panela

1 firm avocado

1 English cucumber or 3 Persian cucumbers

1 sliced jalapeño

3 tablespoons chopped cilantro

1 tablespoon toasted sesame seeds

Finishing salt

Tortilla chips (homemade, page 43, or store-bought), for serving

Tostadas, for serving

In a small bowl, combine the soy sauce, lime juice, orange juice, rice vinegar, and sesame oil. Stir until fully mixed, then add the kosher salt.

Add the sliced red onion to the mix and let it marinate while you prepare the other ingredients.

Slice the Halloumi, avocado, cucumber, and jalapeño into thin slices.

On a platter, layer one portion each of cucumber, Halloumi, sesame seeds, cilantro, jalapeño slices, marinated red onion, and avocado. Repeat until all ingredients are used, finishing off with cilantro, onions, and sesame seeds on top and a dash of finishing salt.

Let it sit for 5 to 10 minutes before serving with tortilla chips or tostadas so the flavors can come together.

NOTES

- *If you want to make it vegan, replace the Halloumi with palm hearts or sliced silken tofu.*
- *If you wish to give this dish a twist, pan fry the Halloumi before building the tiradito.*

TORTITAS DE PAPA Y MASA CON TARTAR DE JALAPEÑOS EN VINAGRE

Potato Masa Harina Patties with Pickled Jalapeño Tartar Sauce

Potatoes and masa are found on menus all across Mexico. No matter where you are, that combination of flavors is always there. Throughout this book, you'll see them pop up in all sorts of delicious and creative ways. As you can imagine, it's one of my all-time favorite combinations.

During my fully vegan years, it actually saved me—whenever I went out to eat, I knew I could always find something satisfying made with potatoes and masa.

And just a heads-up: In Mexico, quesadillas don't always come with cheese! I know it sounds confusing, but you can totally order a quesadilla filled with just potatoes. It's usually a corn tortilla, folded and fried until crispy, with a soft and flavorful papa filling inside. Simple, comforting, and so good. These patties are easy to make and perfect for entertaining. I am serving them here with a pickled jalapeño tartar but feel free to add your favorite salsa or guacamole.

SERVES 8

3 or 4 Yukon Gold potatoes or 2 small russet potatoes (about 2 cups when cooked)

1 tablespoon kosher salt

1 teaspoon onion powder

1 teaspoon garlic powder

½ cup masa harina

½ cup warm water

¼ cup crumbled cotija cheese, optional

½ cup vegetable oil, for frying

For the pickled jalapeño tartar sauce

½ cup mayonnaise (plant-based if vegan)

3 tablespoons finely chopped pickled jalapeños (homemade, page 27, or store-bought)

1 tablespoon pickled jalapeño brine

2 tablespoons chopped capers

2 tablespoons finely chopped red onion or shallot

3 tablespoons chopped fresh cilantro, dill, parsley, or a combination of all

Kosher salt

Freshly ground black pepper

Cook the potatoes in salted water until tender. Be generous with the salt—this is your chance to season them from the inside out.

Let the potatoes cool slightly so they're easier to handle. Then peel and mash them until smooth. Season with the salt, onion powder, and garlic powder.

In a separate bowl, prepare the masa by mixing the masa harina with the warm water until a soft dough forms.

Combine the mashed potatoes with the masa and the cotija cheese, if using. Mix until fully incorporated. The dough should feel soft but hold its shape.

Grab about 1⁄4 cup of the mix and form the patties with your hands, pressing them gently to create even rounds about 4 inches in diameter and 1⁄2 inch thick.

Heat a 10-inch frying pan over medium heat and add the vegetable oil. Fry the patties until crisp and golden on one side, 3 to 4 minutes.

Flip carefully and cook the other side until evenly browned and crispy. Place on a wire rack or a baking sheet lined with paper towels to drain.

To make the pickled jalapeño tartar sauce, in a small bowl, mix the mayonnaise, jalapeños, brine, capers, red onion, and herbs. Stir until well combined. Season to taste with salt and pepper.

Let sit for 5 to 10 minutes for the flavors to meld (or chill for later).

Serve the patties topped with a dollop of the tartar.

NOTE

- *This recipe can be served as lunch, dinner, or an appetizer. If you are serving it as your main, make the patties bigger. If you are making it as an appetizer or botana, make them smaller.*

CEVICHE DE MANZANA VERDE

Green Apple Ceviche

One year, my husband surprised me with a trip to Punta Mita. We stayed at a gorgeous, modern hotel that offered the most extraordinary service and had fun details everywhere. One of my favorite parts of the hotel was a vintage VW Kombi van transformed into a cevichería. The ceviches were unlike anything I had ever seen: elegant foams, unexpected ingredients, and flavor combinations that were completely new to me.

However, they still felt fresh, suitable for eating at the beach, and true to Mexican cuisine. It was there that we tried a green apple ceviche for the first time—and it was love at first bite.

This is my version of that unforgettable dish. It's not fancy or filled with culinary tricks. It's simple, fresh, and easy to make at home. Think of it as the cozy, home-cooked version of something that once felt wildly out of reach—but just as delicious.

SERVES 4

For the dressing

3 tablespoons chopped shallot

¼ cup lime juice

¼ cup orange juice (not too sweet)

¼ cup olive oil

1 jalapeño or serrano, chopped

1 teaspoon kosher salt

For the ceviche

1 small green apple (Granny Smith works great here)

1 English or Persian cucumber

1 avocado

¼ cup fresh cilantro

1 cup sliced hearts of palm or 1 (14-ounce) can

For serving

Corn tostadas or tortilla chips (homemade, page 43, or store-bought)

Start by making the dressing. In a bowl, mix the shallot, lime juice, orange juice, olive oil, sliced chile, and the salt. Let it rest for a few minutes while you prepare the remaining ingredients.

To make the ceviche, dice the apple into small, even cubes (remove the core and seeds but leave the skin on for texture and tartness). You will need about 1 cup. Dice the cucumber, also keeping the skin on. You will need about 1 cup. Dice the avocado. Place the apple, cucumber, and avocado in a large bowl. Add the cilantro and the hearts of palm. Combine all the ingredients and pour in the dressing. Toss everything together and let it chill for 10 minutes. Serve with corn tostadas.

NOTES

- *Buy the whole palmitos and slice them yourself; the presliced hearts of palmito do not hold their shape well.*
- *This would also be a fantastic base to add lime-cooked shrimp or fish.*

LA COMIDA

LUNCH AND DINNER

In Mexican culture, the main meal is at midday, usually between 2:00 and 3:00 p.m. Growing up, we ate dinner as a family at least once a week. The table was always properly set, and in the center was freshly made salsa, corn tortillas that kept coming from the griddle to the table, agua fresca, and sliced avocado. Our meals were always three-course ones. We always had an entrée, soup or a salad, and dessert. During the week, dessert was always something light like fruit or ate de membrillo (quince paste) with cheese, and we all stayed there until my parents finished and we were dismissed, but not without thanking the food and the hands that made it.

We also have meriendas. A Mexican merienda is a light meal that usually takes place between la comida (lunch) and la cena (dinner), often enjoyed during the late afternoon or early evening. It is a time to gather with friends or family, relax, and share a bite as you catch up. It is also called a cafecito. During this time, something light is served, like a quiche or a hearty salad, followed by a sweet treat like brownies, cookies, or a galette.

Then comes la cena, which refers to the evening meal or dinner, typically eaten between 8 and 10 p.m., depending on the region and personal preferences. Cena recipes are both light and easy to make, such as a quick quesadilla, some easy taquitos, or a sandwich. They come together quickly but are flavorful and satisfying.

In this chapter, you'll find recipes that work beautifully for both lunch and dinner. I created them with the rhythm of a typical day in mind—dishes that reflect what we'd naturally eat throughout the day in a Mexican home.

ENSALADA DE MANGO Y QUINOA CRUJIENTE CON ADEREZO DE LIMÓN Y JALAPEÑO

Mango Avocado Salad with Lime Jalapeño Dressing and Crispy Quinoa

Sweet, spicy, creamy, and crunchy—this mango avocado salad has it all. It is inspired by the vibrant flavors I grew up with, and then all tossed in a zesty lime jalapeño dressing and finished with crispy quinoa for that perfect crunch. Make it your own: Serve it with grilled protein, pile it next to your favorite tacos, or enjoy it just as it is. It's light, fresh, and guaranteed to disappear quickly.

SERVES 6

¼ cup olive oil

¼ cup unflavored regular or vegan yogurt

¼ cup lime juice

1 jalapeño, roughly chopped

1 garlic clove

1 teaspoon agave or honey

1 teaspoon kosher salt

3 romaine lettuce heads

¼ cup thinly sliced red onion or Cebollas en Vinagre (page 28)

3 Persian cucumbers, chopped

1 mango, cubed

1 avocado, cubed

1 cup crispy quinoa

Start by making the dressing. In a blender or small food processor, combine the olive oil, yogurt, lime juice, jalapeño, garlic, agave, and salt. Blend until smooth and creamy. Taste and adjust the seasoning if needed.

Chop the romaine lettuce into bite-size pieces and place it in a large bowl. Add the red onion, cucumbers, mango, and avocado. Drizzle the dressing over the salad and gently toss to coat everything evenly. Just before serving, sprinkle the crispy quinoa on top for added crunch.

Serve immediately.

NOTES

- *To make the jalapeño dressing milder, start with half a jalapeño and taste before adding more. For even less heat, remove the seeds and membranes before blending.*
- *In a pinch, mayonnaise or vegan mayo can replace the yogurt. Greek yogurt also works with this dressing.*
- *To make crispy quinoa, start with 1 cup of cooked quinoa—cold or leftover works best. If the quinoa is freshly cooked, spread it out on a plate or baking sheet to cool and dry slightly; the drier it is, the crispier the result.*
- *For the stovetop method, heat a nonstick or cast-iron skillet over medium heat. Add 1 to 2 teaspoons of olive or avocado oil, then spread the quinoa in a single layer. Let it sit undisturbed for 3 to 4 minutes before stirring occasionally until golden and crispy, which usually takes about 10 minutes.*
- *For a larger batch, use the oven. Preheat to 400°F (200°C), toss the quinoa with oil and a pinch of salt, spread it in a thin layer on a parchment-paper-lined baking sheet, and bake for 20 to 25 minutes, stirring halfway through.*
- *You can also use an air fryer by tossing the quinoa with oil and cooking it at 375°F (190°C) for 10 to 12 minutes, shaking halfway. Avoid overcrowding the pan or tray. Once the quinoa is completely cool, store it in an airtight jar to keep it crispy.*

ENSALADA DE KALE Y GARBANZOS CON VINAGRETA DE CHILE ANCHO, NUECES ENCHILADAS Y CEBOLLITA MORADA ENCURTIDA

Kale and Chickpea Salad with Chile Ancho Vinaigrette, Chili-Lime Nuts, and Pickled Red Onions

Don't you love it when you go to a salad restaurant and get an extra-loaded salad in a container that you get to shake, shake, shake to mix all the ingredients and get a heavenly bite? I love it every time, especially with this loaded salad made at home with all the deliciousness of Mexican flavors and different textures.

SERVES 6

For the vinaigrette

1 medium chile ancho (soaked in hot water until soft and pliable)

¼ cup lemon juice

1 tablespoon maple syrup

1 garlic clove

¼ cup olive oil

¼ cup vegetable oil

1 teaspoon kosher salt

For the salad

3 cups stemmed and chopped kale, or a mix of greens of your choice

2 cups spring mix, loosely fitted

1½ cups cooked chickpeas or 1 (15-ounce) can, strained and rinsed

¼ cup fresh cilantro, coarsely chopped

1 cup cherry tomatoes, halved

¼ cup pumpkin seeds (pepitas), preferably roasted

Nueces Picosas con Tajín (page 91)

Cebollas en Vinagre (page 28)

½ cup crumbled cotija cheese or vegan feta cheese

To make the vinaigrette, remove the stem and seeds from the softened chile and then blend it in a blender or food processor with the lemon juice, maple syrup, garlic, olive oil, vegetable oil, and salt until smooth.

To make the salad, toss the chopped kale with a small amount of the vinaigrette and massage until tender.

Add the spring mix, chickpeas, cilantro, tomatoes, pumpkin seeds, nuts, and onions to the kale.

Drizzle more vinaigrette over the salad, toss everything together, finish with the crumbled cheese, and serve.

NOTE

- *Like my other salads, please add your preferred protein to make a larger meal.*
- *When developing this recipe, I tested it using only olive oil and only vegetable oil. Both worked well, but the flavor felt perfectly balanced when I used half olive oil and half vegetable oil. That said, if you prefer to use just one type of oil, it will still work beautifully.*

ENSALADA PICADA CON ADEREZO DE CHIPOTLE Y TAHINI

Chopped Salad with Chipotle Tahini Dressing

The chipotle tahini dressing transforms the simple crunch of raw vegetables into something extraordinary. Creamy, smoky, and just the right amount of spicy, it brings every bite to life. Add your favorite protein to turn this into a satisfying main dish or keep it light and serve it as a refreshing side. And don't stop at salads—this dressing is just as amazing drizzled over roasted veggies or served as a dip for crudités or chips.

SERVES 6

For the chipotle tahini dressing

2 chipotles in adobo sauce

1 tablespoon adobo sauce

2 heaping tablespoons tahini paste

1 garlic clove

3 tablespoons lime juice

⅓ cup olive oil

½ cup ice water

2 teaspoons kosher salt

For the salad

1 ear corn, shucked, silks removed

3 small romaine heads, chopped

1 large English or 3 Persian cucumbers, thinly sliced

10 ounces cherry tomatoes, halved

1 large avocado, diced

1 (15-ounce) can black beans, drained and rinsed or 1½ cups home-cooked black beans, drained

5 ounces (1½ to 2 cups) slightly crumbled tortilla chips (homemade, page 43, or store-bought)

¼ cup crumbled cotija cheese or vegan feta cheese

2 tablespoons chopped cilantro

To make the dressing, place all the ingredients in a blender or food processor. Blend until creamy, pausing halfway to scrape down the sides with a spatula.

To make the salad, heat a large skillet over medium-high heat. Add the whole ear of corn to the skillet. Cook the corn for 10 to 15 minutes, occasionally turning, until it is charred on all sides. Remove it from the skillet and let it cool for a few minutes. Slice off the corn kernels with a sharp knife by holding the ear of corn upright on a cutting board starting at the top of the ear and carefully cutting downward.

To assemble the salad, spread the lettuce on a platter. Add the cucumber, cherry tomatoes, avocado, beans, and grilled corn kernels. Drizzle the dressing over the salad and finish it with tortilla chips, crumbled cotija cheese, and cilantro.

NOTES

- *For a vegan version using vegan feta cheese, if you wish for more protein, add grilled tofu. You could also substitute black beans for chickpeas, or add them as an option.*
- *Add 2 cups of shredded cooked or rotisserie chicken. This salad goes amazingly well with grilled chicken, steak, or salmon.*

BRÓCOLI ROSTIZADO CON CHORIZO CRUMBLE

Roasted Broccoli with Chorizo Crumble

My husband grew up eating bland, flavorless, and overcooked broccoli. When I met him, he said he would eat anything under the sun except broccoli. So, I forged a pact with myself to make him like it. My secret weapon? Roasted broccoli. Now I am sure that this flavorful recipe, with so many different textures and layers of flavor, will transform any not-broccoli enthusiast into a broccoli fan at the first bite.

SERVES 4

For the roasted broccoli

12 ounces broccoli florets, cut into bite-size pieces

Olive oil, for drizzling

Kosher salt

For the chorizo crumbs

4 ounces chorizo, vegan or regular

2 tablespoons vegetable oil (if using vegan chorizo)

1 cup panko

½ teaspoon kosher salt, or more depending on the chorizo

For the avocado crema

1 avocado

2 to 3 tablespoons lime juice

1 garlic clove

1 teaspoon kosher salt

To make the roasted broccoli, preheat the oven to 400°F (200°F).

While the oven heats, toss the broccoli with the olive oil on a baking sheet and season with salt. Spread the broccoli out and roast it for 20 to 25 minutes, or until it's tender and crisp.

To make the chorizo crumbs, heat a large 10-inch skillet over medium-high heat.

If using traditional chorizo, cook it directly in the skillet, breaking it up with the back of a wooden spoon, until browned and cooked through.

If using vegan chorizo, add the oil to the skillet before adding the chorizo. Cook, breaking it up with a wooden spoon, until heated through and lightly browned.

Once the chorizo is cooked, add the panko and kosher salt to the skillet. Cook, stirring frequently, until the breadcrumbs are golden brown, 2 to 3 minutes. Transfer the mixture to a bowl.

To make the crema, cut the avocado in half, remove the pit, and scoop the flesh into a personal blender (such as a Beast or nutribullet) or a small food processor. Add the lime juice, garlic, and salt. Blend until the sauce becomes smooth. If the crema is too thick, add 1 to 2 tablespoons of water.

Spread the avocado crema onto a platter, spoon the roasted broccoli on top, and finish with the chorizo crumbs.

NOTE

- *If you have leftover chorizo crumbs, sprinkle them over pasta, avocado toast, or roasted vegetables.*

GORDITAS DE FRIJOL CON MENTA Y SERRANO

Black Bean, Mint, and Chile Serrano Gorditas

Gorditas are like chubby tortillas—thicker, heartier, and perfect for stuffing with your favorite guisado. Most people know the classic corn version, but there are so many ways to make them: Some are red, some are sweet and made with all-purpose flour, some have beans in the dough, and some are stuffed with cheese. This is my take made with beans, mint, and a little heat from serrano. It is super simple, satisfying, and very customizable.

MAKES 10 TO 12 GORDITAS

2 cups masa harina

2 teaspoons kosher salt, plus more as needed

1¼ cups water

2 tablespoons olive oil

1 (15-ounce) can black beans, drained and rinsed

3 tablespoons chopped fresh mint

2 serrano or jalapeño peppers, finely chopped

For serving

Guacamole of choice (page 32)

Shredded lettuce

Crema or Crema de Cashews (page 34)

Salsa of choice

In a large bowl, whisk together the masa harina and salt. Gradually pour in the water and oil, mixing with your hands or a spoon. The masa may seem dry or crumbly.

Gently fold in the beans, mint, and serrano. Mix until evenly incorporated and a soft, pliable dough forms—similar to the texture of Play-Doh. Slowly add more water if needed.

Cover the bowl with a clean kitchen towel and let the dough rest for 10 or up to 30 minutes.

Divide the dough into 10 to 12 equal portions and roll each one into a ball, about the size of a golf ball. Working with one ball at a time, flatten it into a disc 4 to 5 inches wide and ⅛ to ¼ inch thick. Do this by placing the ball in the palm of one hand and gently pressing it with three fingers of your other hand, turning as you go to keep the shape even.

Heat a comal, griddle, or skillet over medium heat. Place the gorditas on the hot surface and cook for 5 to 6 minutes per side, until golden-brown spots appear and they're cooked through. For a crispier texture, lightly pan fry the cooked gorditas in a bit of oil until golden and slightly crunchy on the outside.

Using a sharp knife, slice each gordita halfway through to create a pocket. Be careful not to cut all the way through. Fill with guacamole, shredded lettuce, crema, and your favorite salsa.

NOTE

- *These gorditas are fantastic filled with melty cheese for a comforting queso gordita. Or try them stuffed with your favorite guisado like picadillo, cortadillo, or even scrambled eggs for a breakfast bite.*

CHILE ANCHO RELLENO DE FRIJOL CON QUESO EN SALSA VERDE

Cheese and Bean-Stuffed Chiles Ancho in Salsa Verde

This is one of the easiest dishes I've ever made, and I'm confident that you'll feel the same way when you try it. The best part is that the chiles look really fancy and have an amazing flavor; it's like experiencing the essence of Mexican cuisine in a single dish. You have the chiles, tomatillos, and beans, which all come together beautifully. There's color, texture, flavor, and simplicity.

SERVES 6

6 big tomatillos, peeled and rinsed

½ medium white onion

1 or 2 chiles (serrano or jalapeño)

3 garlic cloves

½ bunch cilantro

2 teaspoons kosher salt

1 cup water or vegetable broth

2 cups Frijolitos Refritos (page 37) or refried beans of choice

6 chiles ancho

6 pieces of melty cheese cut into sticks, 3 to 4 inches long and ¼ to ½ inch thick (similar in size and shape to a carrot stick)

2 tablespoons vegetable oil

Add the tomatillos, onion, chile serrano, garlic, cilantro, salt, and water to a medium pot. Turn the heat to medium and cook for 10 to 15 minutes, or until the tomatillos are tender and fall apart. Blend the mixture with the cooking liquid until smooth. Set aside.

Warm the refried beans and set aside.

In the meantime, soak the chiles ancho in boiling water until they become pliable. Let them cool and carefully open them in the middle, being cautious not to cut all the way through, then remove the seeds.

Carefully add 2 to 3 tablespoons of the refried beans and 1 piece of cheese, and close the chile. Repeat this process for all of the anchos.

In a large skillet or braiser over medium-low heat, heat the oil and add the reserved salsa, then let it cook for 5 minutes, allowing it to begin simmering.

With the open side facing up, place the chiles in the salsa, cover, and allow them to warm and melt the cheese.

NOTES

- *The chiles must be partially submerged in the salsa. Serve over Arroz Blanco (page 35) or tortilla chips and drizzle with extra salsa.*
- *For a vegan version, I recommend the Violife block cheeses.*

TAQUITOS DE ZANAHORIA

Ricotta, Carrot, and Herb Taquitos with Salsa Verde Cruda

This is one of the easiest dinners you can make. In Mexico, these tacos are very common and usually made with requesón—a soft, fresh cheese like ricotta but slightly drier and crumblier. I decided to use ricotta instead, since it's easier to find—but I've also made them with crumbled tofu, and they turn out great. These tacos are best served with Salsa Verde Cruda, which contrasts perfectly with the sweetness of the carrots. If you do find requesón, definitely use it!

SERVES 4 TO 6

1 cup ricotta cheese or 1 cup pressed and crumbled firm tofu

1½ cups finely grated carrot (about 2 medium carrots)

½ cup finely diced white onion

¼ cup chopped fresh parsley or cilantro

2 teaspoons kosher salt

16 corn tortillas (homemade, page 40, or store-bought)

Vegetable oil for pan frying or baking spray for baking

For serving

Salsa Verde Cruda (page 23)

In a medium bowl, combine the ricotta, carrot, onion, and parsley. Season with salt, then mix well until the ingredients are evenly combined.

Warm the tortillas until they are soft and pliable (either in the microwave, wrapped in a damp towel, for 30 seconds or lightly on a hot skillet) to prevent cracking when rolling.

Place 1½ to 2 tablespoons of filling on the lower third of each tortilla. Roll tightly into a taquito and place seam-side down on a plate. Use a toothpick to secure if needed.

To pan fry

Heat a thin layer of oil in a skillet over medium heat. Fry the taquitos seam-side down first, until golden and crispy, turning as needed, 5 to 7 minutes.

To bake

Preheat the oven to 425°F (220°C). Place the taquitos on a parchment-paper-lined baking sheet, seam-side down. Lightly brush or spray with oil. Bake for 25 to 30 minutes, until golden and crispy.

My favorite way to serve them is with Salsa Verde Cruda, but they also pair nicely with Salsa Verde (page 20), Salsa Roja de Todos los Días (page 19), or any salsa that's your favorite, and if you want them creamier add a drizzle of crema or Crema de Cashews (page 34).

NOTE

- *Make sure to season generously—you want your tacos to be savory, not sweet.*

QUESADILLA CON KIMCHI PICO

Crispy Edge Quesadilla with Kimchi Pico de Gallo

I can't really take credit for the idea behind this recipe. It all started during a trip to Barcelona, where we had dinner at this very avant-garde restaurant—fancy, cool, plant-forward, just a really inspiring mix of things. My daughter, who was younger at the time, was craving something familiar for a meal. Her eyes lit up when she spotted a quesadilla on the menu, but it had kimchi.

As adventurous as she is, she ordered it and loved it. Of course, we all had to try it too. It was such an interesting combination of flavors, and honestly, we were hooked. The only comment we all had as a family was that we wished it had felt a bit fresher.

That's when the idea hit me: Mix the kimchi with avocado. It brightens everything and makes the kimchi quesadilla of my dreams: bold, tangy, creamy, and fresh all in one bite.

MAKES 2 QUESADILLAS

For the kimchi pico de gallo

½ cup finely chopped kimchi

¼ cup thinly sliced scallions, white and green parts

2 teaspoons toasted sesame oil

Pinch of kosher salt

1 ripe avocado, diced

1 tablespoon black sesame seeds

For the quesadillas

1 tablespoon avocado oil or vegetable oil, divided

2 large flour tortillas

1 cup loosely measured shredded cheese (like mozzarella, Oaxaca, or Monterey Jack, or vegan), divided

To make the kimchi pico de gallo, in a small bowl, combine the kimchi, scallions, sesame oil, and salt. Gently fold in the diced avocado and sprinkle with black sesame seeds. Set aside while you make the quesadillas.

Heat a nonstick skillet over medium heat and add half the oil. Place one tortilla in the skillet and sprinkle ½ cup of cheese over half of it. Fold the tortilla over to create a half-moon shape.

Cook for 3 to 4 minutes per side, pressing down slightly and letting the cheese melt and crisp at the edges. Repeat with the remaining 1½ teaspoons of oil, second tortilla, and ½ cup of remaining cheese.

Slice each quesadilla in half and top generously with kimchi pico de gallo.

NOTES

- *For extra-crispy edges, let a little cheese spill out of the tortilla and crisp directly on the pan.*
- *Add a handful of spinach or sautéed mushrooms inside the quesadilla for extra veggies.*
- *For a spicier dish, add a few slices of jalapeño to the kimchi pico de gallo or a drizzle of sriracha before serving.*

TACOS DORADOS DE CAMOTE CON MISO

Crispy Sweet Potato Tacos with Miso

These crispy sweet potato tacos are salty, savory, a little sweet, and packed with umami flavor. The slaw adds the perfect crunch and brightness, making each bite completely satisfying. They're easy to make, perfect for weeknights, and come together faster than you'd expect.

This recipe was inspired by a moment that truly took my breath away. When I walked into one of Gabriela Cámara's restaurants in Mexico City's Centro Histórico, I felt like I had stepped into a space where two of my worlds collided—photography and food. The restaurant is housed in what was once the home of Manuel Álvarez Bravo, one of Mexico's most celebrated twentieth-century photographers. His black-and-white images adorn the exposed brick walls, filling the space with history, art, and a sense of magic.

There, my husband ordered a charred sweet potato dish meant to be turned into tacos with bone marrow and the most perfect salsa. Every dish we tried was beautifully composed, a play of textures and flavors that lingered with us long after. That meal inspired me to create a version at home, simple but bold, cozy but exciting. These tacos are my tribute to that unforgettable experience.

SERVES 4 TO 6

For the sweet potato filling

2 medium sweet potatoes

2 tablespoons neutral oil (avocado or grapeseed)

1 teaspoon kosher salt, plus more as needed

Freshly ground black pepper

1½ tablespoons white miso paste

1 tablespoon soy sauce or tamari, optional (use if the sweet potatoes are very sweet)

For the cabbage slaw

2 cups thinly sliced red or green cabbage

¼ medium red onion, very thinly sliced

1 jalapeño, thinly sliced (remove seeds for less heat)

Juice of 1 lime

1 tablespoon olive oil or avocado oil

3 tablespoons sesame seeds

Pinch of kosher salt

¼ cup chopped cilantro

For the taco assembly

16 corn tortillas (homemade, page 40, or store-bought)

Neutral oil

For serving

Extra lime wedges

Hot sauce, optional

Continued >>

To make the sweet potato filling, preheat the oven to 425°F (220°C). Line a baking sheet with parchment paper.

Lightly rub the sweet potatoes with oil and season with salt and pepper. Pierce each sweet potato 5 or 6 times with a fork. Roast whole, unpeeled, on the prepared baking sheet for 45 to 55 minutes, turning once halfway through, until a knife slides in easily with no resistance and the skins are lightly puffed and wrinkled.

While the sweet potatoes roast, make the cabbage slaw. Combine the cabbage, red onion, jalapeño, lime juice, oil, sesame seeds, and salt in a large bowl. Toss well and let sit for 10 to 15 minutes. Stir in the chopped cilantro just before serving.

Once the sweet potatoes are roasted and cool enough to handle, peel and place them in a bowl. Add the miso paste, soy sauce (if using), and a good pinch of salt. Mash until smooth and well combined. Taste and adjust seasoning—it should be salty, sweet, and full of flavor.

Warm the corn tortillas in a dry skillet, microwave, or directly over a flame until soft and pliable. Keep them warm with a clean kitchen towel.

Fill each tortilla with about 2 tablespoons of the sweet potato filling, fold in half, and place on a baking sheet. Lightly spray or brush the tops with oil. Cook the tacos in an air fryer or skillet.

To cook in an air fryer, preheat to 400°F (200°C). Air fry the tacos for 5 to 6 minutes, or until they are crispy and golden. For the skillet method, heat a bit of oil in a skillet and cook the tacos on each side until golden and crispy.

Serve the tacos hot, topped with a generous spoonful of the cabbage slaw. Add a squeeze of lime and hot sauce, if desired.

NOTE

- *If you'd like to shorten the cooking time, peel and cut the sweet potatoes into evenly sized chunks, toss with olive oil, salt, and pepper, and spread in a single layer without crowding (use two pans if needed). Roast at 400°F (200°C) for 25 to 30 minutes, flipping halfway through, until very tender.*

TOSTADAS DE PAPA Y CHORIZO

Potato Chorizo Tostadas

This is one of my all-time favorite recipes. It's cozy, satisfying, and incredibly versatile—you can serve it for breakfast, lunch, or dinner. It's also my go-to meal on those nights when I'm this close to ordering takeout because I'm too tired to cook. But somehow, this comes together faster than waiting on delivery. The combination of crispy potatoes, savory chorizo, creamy refried beans, and all the toppings hits every craving—and it never disappoints.

MAKES 12 TOSTADAS

1 tablespoon vegetable oil, optional (for use if cooking vegan chorizo)

12 ounces Mexican chorizo, vegan or regular

3/4 cup chopped white onion

3 medium potatoes, diced, about 2 cups

1 teaspoon kosher salt

1 cup Frijolitos Refritos (page 37)

12 tostada shells

Shredded lettuce or cabbage, for serving

Salsa of choice

Mexican crema or Crema de Cashews (page 34), optional

Crumbled cotija cheese or vegan feta, for finishing

Sliced avocado, optional

In a large skillet over medium heat, add a small amount of oil if using vegan chorizo, and cook the chorizo for 5 minutes, breaking it up with a spoon, until it is browned and fragrant. Stir in the chopped onion and sauté for 3 to 4 minutes, or until translucent and softened.

Add the diced potatoes, season with salt, and lower the heat. Cover with a lid and cook for 10 to 15 minutes, stirring occasionally, until the potatoes are tender and everything is well combined.

While the potatoes cook, warm the frijolitos refritos in a small saucepan or in the microwave until heated through. Spread a layer of warm refried beans on each tostada. Top with a generous spoonful of the potato and chorizo mixture, then finish with shredded lettuce, salsa, crema (if using), crumbled cheese, and avocado slices, if desired.

NOTES

- *To save time, use canned refried beans—just warm them up with a splash of water or broth to loosen them up.*
- *For an even quicker version, swap the diced potatoes for frozen hash browns. They cook fast, get crispy, and soak up all the chorizo flavor beautifully.*
- *To make tostadas at home, lightly brush corn tortillas with oil and bake at 400°F (200°C) for 5 to 8 minutes, flipping halfway through, until golden and fully crisp. You can also pan fry them in a bit (about 1 tablespoon) of oil for 30 to 60 seconds per side for a more traditional texture. Let them cool completely so they crisp as they rest, and sprinkle with salt while still warm. Store-bought ones are also perfect here. And if you are having a hard time finding tostadas, use taco shells, even though the Mexican in me is hurting while I write this.*

ALBONDIGAS EN SALSA DE CHIPOTLE

Meatballs in Chipotle Sauce

These albóndigas vuelan (they disappear) every time I make them. My husband always jokes that one day he hopes to find leftovers in the refrigerator so he can make himself a torta. But, nope, not even a drop of sauce is left when the kids are home. Like I mentioned in the intro, my kids are meat eaters—I'm not—so this is one of those dishes I make with plant-based meat so we can all enjoy the same meal. And the best part? They didn't realize what they were actually eating until way later.

SERVES 4 TO 6

For the salsa

1 (28-ounce) can diced tomatoes or its equivalent in fresh tomatoes (about 4 large tomatoes, or 6 Roma tomatoes)

½ medium onion, yellow or white, cut into pieces

2 garlic cloves

1 teaspoon kosher salt

2 chipotle peppers in adobo

1 tablespoon vegetable oil

½ teaspoon oregano

1 sprig of cilantro

For the albóndigas

½ cup cooked white rice or Arroz Blanco (page 35)

2 tablespoons milk (plant-based or regular)

2 garlic cloves, minced or pressed

1 teaspoon kosher salt

Freshly ground black pepper

24 ounces (680 grams) plant-based ground beef substitute or ground beef

To make the salsa, place the tomatoes, onion, garlic, salt, and chipotle peppers in a blender and blend until smooth. Pour the sauce into a large skillet or pot with the oil, then add the oregano and sprig of cilantro. Simmer over medium heat for 6 to 8 minutes, until the sauce deepens in color and slightly thickens.

Meanwhile, in a large bowl, make the albóndigas. Combine the cooked rice and milk and let it sit for at least 5 minutes. Add the minced garlic, salt, and black pepper to taste, then mix well. Add the ground beef. Mix gently with your hands until just combined, being careful not to overwork the mixture.

Form the albóndigas into 1½-inch balls. Once the sauce is ready, gently place the meatballs into the skillet. Reduce the heat to medium-low and cook, uncovered, for 15 to 20 minutes, carefully flipping them halfway through and spooning sauce over the top as they cook. Serve hot with rice, tortillas, or your favorite side.

NOTE

- *If making this recipe with plant-based ground beef and it is a bit soft to hold its shape, add 2 tablespoons of breadcrumbs to the mix.*

CHILES POBLANOS EN HOJALDRE CON ARROZ, CREMA, Y QUESO

Puff Pastry-Wrapped Poblano Peppers

Flaky, golden puff pastry wrapped around roasted poblano peppers stuffed with creamy Mexican rice, cheese, and corn—perfect for a showstopping main dish or appetizer. The inspiration for this dish came from the beloved Mexican rice and poblano casserole. This is a hearty dish that you can serve as dinner or lunch with a big salad on the side and call it a day.

SERVES 6

2 cups cooked Arroz Blanco (page 35)

1 cup diced onion

1 cup corn (frozen or fresh)

2 tablespoons Mexican crema or Crema de Cashews (page 34)

1½ cup shredded cheese (Monterey Jack, mozzarella, Chihuahua or vegan melty cheese)

2 teaspoons kosher salt

6 small or 4 large poblano peppers

1 package of puff pastry, cut into 1½-inch-wide strips

1 egg (for egg wash) or 4 tablespoons cashew or soy milk mixed with 2 teaspoons maple syrup

Preheat the oven to 400°F (200°C). Line a baking sheet with parchment paper.

In a large bowl, combine the cooked rice, diced onion, corn, crema, shredded cheese, and salt. Mix well until creamy and fully combined.

Roast the poblano peppers directly over a flame or under the broiler until charred on all sides.

Place them in a bowl and cover for 10 minutes to steam. Peel off the skin, make a slit, and carefully remove seeds and veins without breaking the pepper.

Gently open each poblano and stuff it with the creamy rice mixture. Close them carefully to keep the filling inside.

Wrap each pepper with strips of puff pastry, creating a mummy-like pattern, leaving small gaps for the filling to peek through. Brush with egg wash for a golden finish.

Place each stuffed poblano on the prepared baking sheet. Bake for 20 to 25 minutes or until the puff pastry is puffed and golden brown.

NOTE

- *Check the ingredient list on the puff pastry, as some brands contain butter. If you need the recipe to be vegan, choose a vegan puff pastry.*

ENCHILADAS SUIZAS ROJAS

Red Enchilada Sauce

In Mexico, enchiladas suizas are usually verdes—green and creamy. But this red version might just be my favorite. The rich, vibrant tomato-chile sauce is bursting with flavor and pairs beautifully with just about any filling you have on hand. It's comforting, colorful, and endlessly versatile—perfect for using up leftovers or making something special from scratch.

SERVES 6 TO 8

½ medium white onion

3 garlic cloves

28 ounces tomato, fresh or canned

3 chipotle peppers in adobo sauce

½ roasted red bell pepper, from a jar

¾ cups sour cream, Mexican cream, or Crema de Cashews (page 34)

2 teaspoons kosher salt

2 tablespoons vegetable oil

12 (6-inch) corn tortillas

2 cups cooked potatoes, a mix of cooked lentils and potatoes, or shredded chicken (see note)

1 cup shredded melty cheese of choice

Preheat the oven to 350°F (200°F).

In a dry skillet over medium heat, char the onion and garlic until deeply golden with a few blackened spots. If you're using fresh tomatoes, add them to the skillet and roast until softened and blistered.

Meanwhile, place the chipotle peppers, red bell pepper, canned tomatoes (if using), sour cream, and salt in a blender. Once the onion, garlic, and tomatoes (if using fresh) are nicely charred, add them to the blender and blend everything until completely smooth. Taste the sauce. It should be really flavorful and smoky, not spicy. Add more chipotle peppers if you want more spice.

In the same skillet, heat the vegetable oil. Lightly pan fry the corn tortillas until they're soft and pliable but not crispy. If you'd prefer to skip the oil, wrap the tortillas in a clean kitchen towel and microwave them for about 30 seconds, or until they are soft and flexible.

Carefully pour the blended salsa into the skillet (it might splatter a bit) and let it simmer over medium heat for about 10 minutes, stirring occasionally, until the sauce thickens and the flavors deepen.

To assemble the enchiladas, add 2 to 3 tablespoons of your filling of choice to each tortilla, roll them up, and place them seam-side down on a plate or cutting board.

Using a 9 x13-inch baking dish (or a similar oven-safe dish), spread 1½ to 2 cups of the sauce evenly on the bottom. Arrange the enchiladas in the dish, seam-side down. Pour the remaining sauce over the top and finish with a generous layer of grated cheese.

Bake for 15 to 20 minutes, or until the cheese is melted and the sauce is bubbling.

Serve warm with white rice, refried beans, or roasted vegetables on the side.

NOTE

- *These enchiladas are super versatile and perfect for using up leftovers. I've made them with just cooked potatoes or a mix of lentils and potatoes, and my husband has even made them with shredded chicken. If you've got leftover carne asada, go for it—shredded pork or diced steak work beautifully too. Use what you have and make them yours.*

PICADILLO, CORTADILLO, AND TINGA

Picadillo, cortadillo, and tinga—these are classic Mexican guisados you'll find in almost every refrigerator across Mexico. We usually make them once a week, and honestly, no one ever gets tired of them. Leftovers? Yes. Boring? Never.

Cortadillo is a dish from northern Mexico, and for me, it's a little homage to the time I spent there. I was born in Mexico City but grew up in Monterrey, where I lived from the age of sixteen until I moved to Texas. This dish is super versatile. Serve it as a main or use it to fill tacos or gorditas. It works beautifully with corn or flour tortillas.

Picadillo is in the same comforting, homey category. My recipe is originally from Mexico City, and we always joke that in CDMX, we turn our picadillo into a salad—we love loading it with vegetables like carrots, peas, and potatoes. It's cozy, satisfying, and full of flavor. You can serve it in tacos, sopes, tostadas, or as a main dish with rice—however you like your leftovers.

And then there's tinga—one of my absolute favorites. I make mine with oyster mushrooms, but you can easily substitute shredded chicken. The process is exactly the same, so feel free to make it your own. And when it comes to leftovers? Get creative. Serve them as tostadas, tacos, over rice, or go big and wrap it all up in a burrito with rice, beans, and your favorite guisado.

Picadillo

Mexican Ground Beef with Potatoes and Vegetables

Picadillo comes from the Spanish word picar, which means "to chop," and it makes perfect sense; this dish is all about small, tender bites of flavorful ingredients. There are many regional variations. Picadillo ranchero is often spicier, with a brothier consistency and chiles; picadillo blanco is made without tomato sauce and has a more delicate flavor profile and both are from the Northern region.

But this version? This is the one I grew up with.

It's the Mexico City kind, full of chopped vegetables, saucy, savory, and comforting. Carrots, potatoes, and peas, all simmered with ground "beef" in a rich tomato sauce. We ate it spooned over white rice, stuffed into tacos, on crispy tostadas, or even wrapped in warm flour tortillas for a quick lunch.

It's simple, satisfying, and so nostalgic—the kind of meal that makes the kitchen feel like home.

SERVES 6

1 tablespoon vegetable oil

1 (12-ounce) package of plant-based ground beef or ground beef

1 small onion, chopped

2 garlic cloves, minced

1 (15-ounce) can tomato sauce or purée

2 carrots, peeled and diced

1 to 2 potatoes, peeled and cut into ½-inch cubes

1 cup frozen peas

½ teaspoon dried thyme

½ teaspoon dried marjoram

1 bay leaf

1 teaspoon kosher salt

In a large skillet, warm the oil and brown the plant-based ground beef over medium heat. Once it's cooked through and starting to crisp up a bit, stir in the onion and garlic for about 3 minutes, until fragrant and just starting to turn golden.

Stir in the tomato sauce, carrots, potatoes, peas, thyme, marjoram, bay leaf, and salt.

Cover and let it simmer for about 20 minutes, or until the potatoes are tender. If the mixture starts to look too dry, add a splash of water to loosen it up. Remove and discard the bay leaf before serving.

NOTE

- *You can also make picadillo with cooked lentils instead of ground beef or plant- based ground beef.*

Continued >>

Cortadillo

Beef and Mushroom Stew in Tomato Sauce

Cortadillo is northern Mexico's answer to a saucy, cozy weeknight guisado—and it's one of those dishes that always reminds me of Monterrey, where I spent most of my teenage years. Unlike bistec a la Mexicana, which is often more sautéed and less saucy, cortadillo is heartier, saucier, and seasoned with a bit of cumin. It's often made with beef, but my version includes sliced mushrooms for extra flavor and texture—and of course, you can keep it vegan with plant-based steak or go traditional with thin-cut beef.

It's a dish meant for tacos, rice bowls, or stuffing into gorditas. It always tastes better the next day, so it's perfect for leftovers.

SERVES 6

2 tablespoons vegetable oil

1 (10-ounce) vegan steak (like Beyond Steak) or ¾ pound thinly diced beef (flank, top round, or sirloin)

1 small white or yellow onion, thinly sliced

8 ounces baby bella (cremini) or white button mushrooms, cleaned and sliced

3 Roma tomatoes, diced or pulsed in a food processor or blender or 1 (14-ounce) can diced tomatoes

2 jalapeños or 1 serrano chile, seeded and diced

1 to 2 garlic cloves, minced, optional

1 teaspoon kosher salt

½ teaspoon ground cumin

Heat the oil in a large skillet over medium-high heat. Add the steak and cook until browned and cooked through, 2 to 5 minutes depending on the type you are using.

Add the sliced onion and mushrooms. Cook for about 2 minutes, until softened and starting to brown slightly. Stir in the tomatoes, jalapeños, garlic (if using), salt, and cumin. Simmer for 3 to 4 minutes, until the mixture becomes saucy and the flavors come together.

Serve with corn or flour tortillas (homemade, page 40, or store-bought), over fluffy Arroz Blanco (page 35), or as a filling for tacos or gorditas. Don't forget the Frijolitos Refritos (page 37) on the side.

Continued >>

Tinga

Shredded Chicken or Mushrooms in Chipotle Tomato Sauce

A smoky, saucy classic, with mushrooms or chicken, tinga is one of those dishes that feels like a warm hug—flavorful and endlessly versatile. I usually make it with shredded oyster mushrooms, but shredded chicken works just as well if that's more your style. The base is a rich chipotle-tomato sauce, made from fresh tomatoes simmered with garlic, and everything comes together in one skillet. It's perfect for tacos, tostadas, burritos, or rice bowls—however you love your guisados.

SERVES 6

4 to 6 ripe tomatoes

2 garlic cloves

2 to 4 chipotle peppers in adobo sauce

1 tablespoon kosher salt (adjust to taste)

2 tablespoons vegetable oil or avocado oil

5 cups oyster mushrooms, shredded, or 2 cups cooked, shredded chicken

1 medium white onion, thinly sliced

1 tablespoon dried oregano

Place the tomatoes and garlic in a saucepan and cover with water. Bring to a boil and simmer for about 10 minutes, just until the tomatoes are soft but not mushy. Drain and set aside to cool slightly.

Add the cooked tomatoes, garlic, chipotle peppers, and salt to a blender. Blend until smooth.

If you are using the oyster mushrooms, heat the oil in a large skillet over medium-high heat. Add the shredded oyster mushrooms and cook for 7 to 8 minutes, stirring occasionally, until golden and tender. Add the sliced onion and sauté for about 5 minutes, until soft and translucent.

If you are using the chicken, heat the oil in a large skillet over medium-high heat. Add the sliced onion and sauté for about 5 minutes, until soft and translucent. Add the shredded chicken and stir to combine.

When either the mushrooms or chicken is ready, pour in the chipotle-tomato sauce, add the dried oregano, and adjust seasoning if needed. Stir everything together and simmer for 10 to 15 minutes.

Serve with warm corn tortillas (homemade, page 40, or store-bought), Arroz Blanco (page 35), and Frijolitos Refritos (page 37).

PARA EL FIN

FOR THE WEEKEND

There's something special about cooking together—whether it's around the kitchen island or out by the grill. In both Mexican and American culture, food isn't just about eating—it's about gathering, connecting, and creating memories. Now that all my kids are grown, one of my favorite things is having everyone back home, chatting, laughing, and cooking side by side. I'll throw together a quick pasta (always with a Mexican twist, like my Pasta con Salsa Macha [page 157]), pour a glass of wine, and just soak in the moment.

The kitchen, to me, is where the best conversations happen—it's where life feels full. My husband always says the best family/friends talks start and end there, and I couldn't agree more. This chapter is all about those kinds of meals—dishes meant to be shared family-style, set up taquiza-style, or laid out as a festive spread where everyone can dig in and feel at home.

FRIJOLES PUERCOS

Piggy Beans

What are frijoles puercos? Think of them as spicy, extra-loaded refried beans, cooked with chorizo, jalapeños, and lots of melty cheese. I know, the name is a little weird (it literally means "piggy beans"), but it's a dish I grew up loving.

My mom is from Sinaloa, where frijoles puercos are a typical party staple. I remember my grandma making them for taquizas; casual parties where different guisados (like stews and fillings) are laid out buffet-style, and everyone builds their own tacos.

When we lived in Mexico City, my parents loved hosting taquizas. Like many families from the city, we had a weekend house in Cuernavaca. So, from the time I was two until we moved to Monterrey, we spent nearly every weekend and many summers there. These beans bring me right back to those weekends: loud conversations, warm tortillas, and food meant to be shared. Serve these beans as a side dish or as a dip with tortilla chips.

SERVES 8

6 ounces Mexican chorizo, vegan or regular

1 tablespoon vegetable oil

3 cups cooked beans, black or pinto beans or 2 (15-ounce) cans, undrained

¾ to 1 cup of water if using home-cooked beans

2 to 4 tablespoons chopped pickled jalapeño peppers (drained, but save the brine)

1 cup grated melty cheese of choice

1 teaspoon kosher salt

In a large skillet over medium heat, cook the chorizo with the vegetable oil for 5 to 6 minutes or until browned.

Place the beans with their liquid in a blender and blend until creamy. If using home-cooked beans, add water to make them run smoothly.

Pour the blended beans over the cooked chorizo, mix, and add the jalapeños. Add the cheese and mix until melted. Season with salt and taste.

If the beans are too thick, you can add the jalapeño brine or more water to loosen them up.

NOTE

- *There's no need to add more spices; Mexican chorizo is quite well seasoned; just use a good one.*

ENSALADA DE TOMATILLO, TOMATITOS Y BURRATA

Burrata, Tomatillo, and Cherry Tomato Salad

When I developed this recipe, I was a bit apprehensive about the combination of flavors. However, everyone in my home loved it. I thought, "Okay, first attempt!" So, I made it again and had my parents try it. They loved it, too. Finally, I sent the recipe to my cousin Paloma, who graciously agreed to help me test some recipes for the cookbook. She lives in Spain, and when I shared my concerns, she reassured me that her Mexican Spanish family enjoyed it as well, even my friend's niece with German heritage. This gave me the reassurance I needed, and I knew this recipe had to be included in the cookbook for sure. Love it as a salad or as a starter with homemade tortilla chips.

SERVES 6

½ small red onion, thinly sliced (about ½ cup)

Zest of 1 lime

3 to 4 tablespoons lime juice (about 2 small limes)

1 teaspoon kosher salt, plus more as needed

3 tablespoons olive oil, plus more for drizzling

1 cup rinsed, peeled, and diced tomatillos

1 cup cherry tomatoes, quartered or chopped to match the size of the tomatillos

½ cup chopped fresh cilantro

¼ cup chopped fresh mint

2 or 3 balls burrata cheese

1 jalapeño, very thinly sliced

½ teaspoon dried oregano

Start by preparing the dressing: In a small bowl, mix the red onion with the lime zest, lime juice, 1 teaspoon salt, and olive oil. Let it sit for 5 to 10 minutes to soften the onion slightly.

On a serving platter, arrange the diced tomatillos and cherry tomatoes. Sprinkle the chopped cilantro and mint over the top, then drizzle with the dressing. Tear open the burrata balls and place them over the salad.

Finish with a drizzle of olive oil, a pinch of salt, the thinly sliced jalapeño, and a sprinkle of dried oregano. Serve immediately.

NOTE

- *If you want this version vegan, skip the fresh burrata and finish with vegan ricotta. For this recipe it is important to use cherry tomatoes or other sweet tomatoes.*

COL ASADA CON ADEREZO DE CASHEW Y LIMÓN

Charred Cabbage with Lime Cashew Crema Dressing

If you've never grilled cabbage before, this is your sign. Charred cabbage is smoky, tender, and surprisingly satisfying, especially when drizzled with a zesty lime cashew crema that brightens up everything it touches. This is the perfect vegetable side when you're hosting a carne asada, it looks beautiful as a family-style dish, and it is delicious. It holds its own next to grilled meats, adds vibrant color to the table, and just feels special. The crema is creamy, citrusy, and totally addictive—you'll want to put it on everything.

SERVES 6

For the cabbage

1 medium green cabbage, cut into 8 wedges (keep the core intact so wedges stay together)

2 tablespoons olive oil

1 teaspoon kosher salt

½ teaspoon freshly ground black pepper

For the lime cashew crema

½ cup raw cashews (soaked in hot water for 20 minutes if not using a high-speed blender)

½ cup water, plus more to thin, if needed

Zest of 1 lime

Juice of 2 limes (about ¼ cup)

1 garlic clove

1 tablespoon olive oil

½ teaspoon kosher salt

For serving

Chopped cilantro

Toasted pistachios or pepitas

Thinly sliced jalapeño, optional

To make the cabbage, preheat a grill or cast-iron skillet over medium-high heat.

Brush the cabbage wedges with olive oil and sprinkle with salt and pepper on all sides.

Place the wedges cut-side down and cook for 5 to 7 minutes per side, or until deeply charred and tender in the center. Flip gently to avoid breaking the wedges.

To make the lime cashew crema, drain the soaked cashews and add them to a blender with the water, lime zest, lime juice, garlic, olive oil, and salt. Blend until smooth and creamy. Adjust the consistency by adding more water and adjust the taste for salt or acidity.

Arrange the charred cabbage on a platter. Drizzle generously with the lime cashew crema. Garnish with chopped cilantro, toasted pistachios, or jalapeño slices if desired. Serve warm or at room temperature.

ESQUITES DE COLECITAS

Grilled Brussels Sprouts Esquites

Esquites are super popular in Mexico—you might know them here in the United States as "street corn." But getting a real esquite in Mexico? That's a whole experience. Usually, there's a street vendor with a giant pot of cooked white corn. Well, actually two pots: one for corn kernels (esquites) and another for corn on the cob (elotes).

Mexican corn is different from the sweet corn you typically find in the United States. It's grainier, sturdier, and full of texture. Back to the vendor—when it's your turn, they'll ask: ¿Con todo? That's the magic phrase. It means, with everything: crema, mayonnaise, lime juice, chili paste, and chile powder. The best combo ever.

I love that flavor so much—it brings back so many memories. And honestly, I've always thought: Why stop at corn? So today, I present you with: roasted Brussels sprouts esquites. Same flavor, unexpected veggie twist. You're going to love them.

SERVES 4

For the Brussels sprouts

6 cups halved or quartered Brussels sprouts, depending on the size

2 tablespoons olive oil or vegetable oil

Kosher salt

For the dressing

3 tablespoons Mexican crema or Crema de Cashews (page 34)

3 tablespoons mayonnaise or vegan mayonnaise

Zest and juice of 1 lime

1 teaspoon kosher salt

1 teaspoon ground chile ancho

Cilantro, for serving

4 ounces cotija cheese or vegan Parmesan or Feta cheese

Oven Method

Preheat the oven to 400°F (200°C). Toss the Brussels sprouts with the oil and salt. Spread evenly on a baking sheet lined with parchment paper. Roast for 20 to 25 minutes, flipping once halfway through, until golden and crispy on the edges.

Air Fryer Method

Preheat the air fryer to 375°F (190°C), if your model requires preheating. Toss the sliced Brussels sprouts in a bowl with the oil and salt. Air fry in a single layer (in batches if needed) for 10 to 12 minutes, shaking the basket or stirring halfway through.

While the Brussels sprouts are roasting, make the dressing by mixing the Mexican crema, mayonnaise, lime zest and juice, and salt with the chile ancho in a small bowl.

Remove the Brussels sprouts from the oven and place them on a large extended platter. Drizzle them with the dressing and finish with cilantro and cotija cheese. These grilled Brussels sprout esquites are best when eaten the same day.

NOTES

- *For extra crispiness, don't overcrowd the pan or air fryer basket.*
- *The dressing should be tangy, not too salty, and creamy with a slight spicy kick at the end of each bite.*

CARNITAS DE CHAMPIÑÓN

Mushroom Carnitas

My great-aunt—a beautiful German woman who, due to the war, arrived in Mexico early in life—lived with my great-grandfather in Huichapan, Hidalgo. We'd visit her from time to time, and every trip was pure magic: German stories, cakes, hearty food . . . and carnitas.

Yes, carnitas. She lived near a spot known for making some of the original Hidalgo-style carnitas (and yes, Hidalgo is indeed one of the traditional birthplaces of carnitas in Mexico). My siblings and I would sneak away from the house with my dad whenever we could to get a delicious taquito. Nothing compares to freshly made tortillas with real corn flavor and carnitas served hot straight from a massive copper pot.

This is my version of that memory made with mushrooms. Easier to prepare, totally plant-based, but still flavorful enough to bring it all rushing back: the smells, the taste, the joy.

SERVES 6 TO 8

2 pounds mushrooms (oyster, king oyster, or of choice)

2 teaspoons instant coffee powder

2 teaspoons garlic powder

2 teaspoons chile powder (ancho or a mix of your favorite Mexican chiles)

2 tablespoons vegetable oil

½ teaspoon ground cumin

¼ cup orange juice

1 tablespoon dried oregano

1 bay leaf

1 tablespoon kosher salt (or ½ tablespoon table salt)

For serving

Corn tortillas (homemade, page 40, or store-bought)

Diced white onion

Cilantro

Salsa of choice

Clean the mushrooms and either shred them with a fork for a pulled texture or cut them into bite-size pieces.

In a large bowl, mix together the instant coffee powder, garlic powder, chile powder, vegetable oil, ground cumin, orange juice, dried oregano, bay leaf, and salt. Stir well.

Add the mushrooms to the bowl and toss until fully coated with the marinade.

While the mushrooms marinate, preheat the oven or air fryer.

Continued >>

Oven Method

Preheat the oven to 425°F (220°C).

Spread the marinated mushrooms evenly on a baking sheet lined with parchment paper. Bake for 20 to 25 minutes, stirring halfway through, until the mushrooms are browned and slightly crispy on the edges.

Air Fryer Method

Preheat the air fryer to 400°F (200°C). Place the marinated mushrooms in the air fryer basket in a single layer (work in batches if needed). Air fry for 12 to 15 minutes, shaking the basket halfway through, until golden brown and slightly crispy.

Remove the bay leaf before serving.

To serve the tacos

Make tacos with the corn tortillas and finish with a squeeze of lime, a sprinkle of diced onion, cilantro, and a spoonful of salsa.

NOTES

- *For extra-crispy carnitas, broil the oven-baked mushrooms for 2 to 3 minutes at the end. Serve in tacos, burritos, bowls, or wherever you would use carnitas.*
- *If the orange juice is too sweet, add a teaspoon of vinegar.*
- *Depending on the type and freshness of the mushrooms, they may release liquid. This is normal; just let them sit a bit longer in the oven until the liquid nearly evaporates. If you're unsure whether your mushrooms will release liquid, bake them on a rimmed baking sheet instead of using an air fryer.*

FLAUTITAS PIÑATERAS DE FRIJOL Y QUESO

Piñata-Style Bean and Cheese Flautas

These crispy flautas are layered with avocado tomatillo salsa, crema, and cotija cheese, just like the ones at every good party back in Mexico.

When we lived in Mexico, every time my kids had a party, especially a birthday, I always hired a flautero. Nothing fancy. Just a guy with a grill making the best flautas on earth. Crispy, golden, and served hot with salsa and cream. The kids loved them! I always ordered more than needed because I loved having extras in the freezer for emergencies or a craving attack.

That memory stuck with me so much that I had to re-create it. These flautas are filled with creamy beans and cheese. Sometimes I serve them upright in a cup over salsa, just like you'd get from a street cart, only more party-friendly.

MAKES 16 FLAUTAS

For the flautas

¾ cup Frijolitos Refritos (page 37)

½ cup shredded cheese (like Oaxaca, Chihuahua, Monterrey Jack or vegan mozzarella)

16 corn tortillas

Oil, for pan frying or oil spray, for air frying

For the avocado tomatillo salsa

1 avocado

4 or 5 tomatillos, peeled, rinsed, and cooked in water until soft, and drained and cooled

½ small white onion

1 to 2 serrano or jalapeño chiles (adjust to taste)

½ cup fresh cilantro

Juice of 1 lime

1 teaspoon kosher salt

For serving

Mexican crema or vegan sour cream

Crumbled cotija cheese

To make the flautas, warm the beans slightly and mix in the shredded cheese. The mixture should be smooth and spreadable.

Heat the tortillas so they're pliable (you can wrap them in a damp towel and microwave for 30 to 60 seconds or heat them on a skillet).

To make the salsa, place the avocado, cooked tomatillos, onion, chile, cilantro, lime juice, and salt in a blender and blend until smooth and creamy.

Add a spoonful of filling to each tortilla, roll tightly, and secure with a toothpick.

Pan Fry Method

Heat oil in a skillet and fry flautas until golden and crispy.

Air Fryer Method

Lightly spray the flautas with oil spray and cook in the air fryer at 400°F (200°C) for 8 minutes, or until golden and crisp.

To serve, drizzle with crema and sprinkle generously with cotija cheese. Offer the salsa on the side.

NOTES

- *You can roll and freeze the uncooked flautas. Just cook straight from frozen and add a few extra minutes to the cooking time.*
- *If you are in a hurry, you can use the tomatillos raw. Just peel and rinse them well before adding to the blender.*

COSTRA JALAPEÑOS TACOS

Stuffed Jalapeño Tacos

In Veracruz, there are some seriously delicious tacos, but the fried jalapeño tacos will always have my heart. I spent years trying to make a vegan version at home, playing around with fillings, batters, and substitutions. These tacos are like a cross between street food and the classic-style chile relleno, the kind coated in fluffy egg white batter and served piping hot.

After lots of trial and error, I decided to keep it simple and let the jalapeño shine. No batter, no deep-frying. Just a fresh chile stuffed with melty cheese, grilled until golden, with the cheese spilling out and forming that irresistible crispy costra.

I eat them just like I remember: wrapped in a warm corn tortilla, topped with guacamole, and that spicy, cheesy, slightly charred chile stealing the show.

MAKES 6 TACOS

6 large jalapeños

1 cup shredded melty cheese, like mozzarella, or vegan version

6 corn tortillas (homemade, page 40, or store-bought)

Guacamole of choice (page 32)

Rinse and dry the jalapeños. Make a lengthwise slit down one side of each pepper, leaving the stem on. Then, make a small horizontal cut just below the stem, forming a "T" shape. Carefully open the pepper and use a small spoon or paring knife to remove the seeds and veins. Be gentle so the jalapeño stays intact.

Fill each jalapeño with shredded cheese. Gently pack it in; it's okay if a bit of cheese spills out.

Heat a nonstick or cast-iron skillet over medium-low heat. Place the stuffed jalapeños, cut-side up, directly onto the hot skillet. Let them cook, undisturbed, for a few minutes until the cheese starts to melt and the chiles brown at the bottom.

If the cheese begins to melt too quickly and the jalapeño isn't softening yet, cover the skillet for 2 to 3 minutes to trap the heat. Then uncover and continue cooking until the cheese oozes out and forms a golden, crispy crust.

On a warm corn tortilla, add a spoonful of guacamole and place 1 cooked jalapeño on top. Cut and discard the stem before serving.

TORTAS AHOGADAS

Drowned Sandwiches

This is a classic from Jalisco, Mexico—crispy bread rolls filled with carnitas, refried beans, and pickled onions, then "drowned" in a tomato broth and topped with a spicy salsa you can dial up or down but please don't skip it, it's part of the magic.

Fair warning: This is going to get messy. It's the kind of dish where you don't know whether to grab a fork and knife or just dive in with your hands. Either way, you won't be able to stop. By the end, you'll find yourself reaching for a million napkins . . . and loving every second of it.

MAKES 4 TORTAS

For the tomato broth

4 Roma tomatoes

¼ small white onion

2 garlic cloves

2 cups water

½ teaspoon oregano

1 teaspoon kosher salt

1 tablespoon vegetable oil

For the salsa picosa (spicy salsa)

¼ cup chile de árbol

¾ cup water (to boil the chiles)

¼ teaspoon dried oregano

⅛ teaspoon ground cumin

⅛ teaspoon freshly ground black pepper

Pinch of allspice

Pinch of ground cloves

1 teaspoon toasted sesame seeds

1 small garlic clove

½ teaspoon kosher salt

¼ teaspoon white vinegar

For assembling

4 crusty bread rolls (like bolillos or telera rolls)

1 cup Frijolitos Refritos (page 37)

1 recipe Mushroom Carnitas (page 145) or about 1 pound of your favorite pulled-pork recipe

Pickled Red Onions (page 28)

2 limes, cut into wedges

To make the tomato broth, place the tomatoes, onion, and garlic in a small saucepan with the water. Bring to a boil and cook until softened. Transfer everything, including the cooking liquid, to a blender. Add the oregano and salt, and blend until smooth.

Continued >>

In the same saucepan, heat the vegetable oil over medium heat. Carefully return the blended broth to the pot and simmer for 3 to 5 minutes, until slightly thickened and deepened in color. Lower the heat and keep warm until ready to use.

To make the salsa, boil the chile de árbol in the water for about 10 minutes. Transfer the chile de árbol to a blender with ¼ cup of the boiling water and add the spices, sesame seeds, garlic, salt, and vinegar and blend until smooth.

To assemble the tortas, slice each roll lengthwise (not all the way through). Spread a layer of frijolitos refritos on one side and add a generous amount of warm carnitas.

Close the roll and pour warm tomato broth over it until it's fully "drowned," about ¾ cup. Top with salsa picosa, pickled onions, and a good squeeze of lime.

NOTES

- *If you can't find telera rolls or bolillos, use a 6- to 7-inch piece of crusty bread instead, such as a baguette.*

PASTA CON CREMA DE POBLANO ESPINACAS Y ALCACHOFAS

Baked Poblano Cream Pasta with Spinach and Artichokes

Creamy, cheesy, and full of flavor, this pasta bake is pure comfort food, but with a little twist.

I took inspiration from the classic espagueti verde we all know and love, but turned it into a baked rigatoni dish. The pasta gets coated in a silky roasted poblano crema, and then it's layered with a ricotta filling loaded with spinach and artichokes—because I'm always looking for ways to sneak in more veggies. It's cozy, satisfying, vegetarian, and has that irresistible green glow that just makes you want to grab a fork.

SERVES 6 TO 8

For the poblano crema

4 poblano peppers

1 cup crema, sour cream, or Crema de Cashews (page 34)

1 cup milk, plant-based or regular

¼ medium white onion

2 garlic cloves

2 teaspoons kosher salt

Freshly ground black pepper

1 pound rigatoni, ziti, or penne pasta

For the spinach and artichoke filling

2 tablespoons olive oil

½ medium onion, finely chopped

4 garlic cloves, finely chopped

16 ounces frozen spinach, thawed and squeezed dry

8 ounces frozen artichoke hearts, thawed and chopped

2 teaspoons kosher salt

Pinch of allspice

For the cheese mixture

16 ounces ricotta cheese or almond ricotta

½ cup crema or Crema de Cashews (page 34)

½ cup freshly grated Parmesan, pecorino cheese, or vegan Parmesan

1 teaspoon kosher salt

1 pound fresh mozzarella or vegan mozzarella, cut into small pieces

Preheat the oven to 375°F (190°C). Line a baking sheet with parchment paper or aluminum foil.

To make the poblano crema, char the poblano peppers under a broiler or over an open flame until blackened all over. Transfer to a bowl and cover tightly with plastic wrap (or place in a sealed plastic bag) to steam for 10 to 15 minutes. Then peel off the charred skin and remove seeds and stems.

In a blender, combine the peeled poblanos, crema, milk, onion, garlic, salt, and black pepper to taste. Blend until completely smooth and creamy.

Bring a large pot of salted water to a boil. Cook the pasta until just shy of al dente; you want it slightly undercooked. Reserve 1 cup of the pasta water before draining. Return the pasta to the cooking pot.

While the pasta cooks, make the spinach-artichoke filling. Heat olive the oil in a large skillet over medium heat. Sauté the onion and garlic until fragrant, about 2 minutes. Add the spinach and artichokes, then season with salt and allspice. Cook until everything is well combined and there is no liquid left. Set aside and let it come to room temperature.

To make the cheese mixture, in a large bowl, combine the ricotta, crema, and Parmesan cheese. Season with salt and fold in the spinach-artichoke mixture.

Add the poblano sauce to the drained pasta and stir to coat. If the sauce is too thick, add some of the reserved pasta water, a little at a time, until it's silky and the pasta is well coated.

In a 3-quart baking dish, layer half of the pasta with sauce. Top with half of the ricotta-spinach-artichoke mixture and half the mozzarella. Add the remaining pasta, making sure to scrape the bowl and transfer all of the poblano sauce into the dish. Top with the remaining ricotta mixture and the rest of the mozzarella.

Place the dish on the prepared baking sheet to catch drips and bake for 30 to 40 minutes, or until bubbly and golden brown on top. Let cool for 10 to 15 minutes before serving.

Serve with a big leafy salad or roasted vegetables for a complete, satisfying meal.

PASTA CON SALSA MACHA

Butter Salsa Macha Pasta

You know that moment—maybe after a party, maybe after your friends just left—and you're not ready for the night to end. You're tipsy, happy, and *hungry*. You need something *more* than just a quesadilla, but are not ready to cook a full tornaboda dish, like chilaquiles. You want something spicy, a little fatty, totally satisfying . . . something that will tuck you into bed with a full belly and a smile on your face.

This is our 3 a.m. pasta dish. It's bold, quick, forgiving, and ridiculously good. Exactly what you want when you're still dancing in your head but also standing over the stove in your pajamas.

SERVES 4

1 pound spaghetti

4 tablespoons (½ stick) butter or vegan butter

4 heaping tablespoons Salsa Macha (page 24) or store-bought

¼ cup chopped parsley, plus more for serving

½ cup grated Parmesan cheese, plus more for serving

Bring a large pot of salted water to a boil. Cook the spaghetti according to the package instructions until it is al dente.

In a large skillet, melt the butter over medium heat. Add the salsa macha and let it cook for 1 to 2 minutes, stirring, until fragrant and slightly foamy (be careful not to burn the chili bits).

Add the cooked pasta directly from the cooking pot to the skillet and toss to coat. If needed, add a splash of the cooking pasta water to help the butter and salsa coat the noodles evenly; make sure they are completely coated.

Remove from the heat and stir in the parsley and the Parmesan. Toss everything together until the cheese melts into the sauce and the pasta is glossy. Taste and adjust with a bit of salt if needed.

Serve immediately, garnished with extra Parmesan and parsley, if desired.

NOTE

- *I use Violife Parmesan cheese for a vegan option.*

TACOS BAJA

Baja Tacos with Beer-Battered Oyster Mushrooms or Cod

Each bite of these tacos takes you straight to heaven and back. The textures, the flavors, everything comes together like a dream. The light beer batter adds just the right crispiness to the tender cod and/or oyster mushrooms, perfectly balanced by the fresh pico and that creamy, smoky chipotle slaw. Crunchy, spicy, tangy, and light all at once, it's the kind of taco you'll crave again and again.

SERVES 4 TO 6

For the slaw

3 tablespoons vegan or regular mayonnaise

1 tablespoon finely chopped chipotle peppers in adobo sauce

2 tablespoons lime juice

Kosher salt

1 small red cabbage, thinly sliced

For the beer batter

2¼ cups all-purpose flour, divided

1 teaspoon baking powder

¼ teaspoon Mexican oregano

2 teaspoons kosher salt, plus more as needed

1 (12-ounce) bottle Mexican light beer (like Corona or Modelo)

2 to 3 cups frying oil

For the protein

14 ounces (400 grams) fresh cod, cut into 1-inch strips

7 ounces (200 grams) oyster mushrooms, cleaned and separated

Kosher salt

For the tacos

12 corn tortillas (homemade, page 40, or store-bought)

Pico de Gallo (page 31)

Lime wedges, for serving

To make the slaw, in a large bowl, combine the mayonnaise, chipotle pepper, lime juice, and salt to taste until smooth and creamy. Add the red cabbage and mix well. Set aside.

To make the batter, in a large bowl, whisk together 1¼ cups of flour, baking powder, oregano, and salt. Gradually pour in the beer, whisking until the batter is thick and smooth, like loose pancake batter.

Place the remaining 1 cup of flour in a shallow dish and season lightly with salt. Heat the oil in a Dutch oven or heavy pan to 350°F (175°C).

If using cod, pat the fish dry and lightly season with salt. Dredge the cod and/or oyster mushrooms in the seasoned flour, shaking off excess. Dip each piece into the beer batter to coat.

Fry in hot oil in batches for 4 to 5 minutes, turning as needed, until golden brown and crispy on both sides. Transfer to a wire rack or a plate lined with paper towels to drain.

To prepare the tacos, warm the tortillas on a skillet or grill. Add 1 or 2 pieces of crispy cod or mushrooms (or a mix!) to each tortilla. Top with a generous spoonful of chipotle slaw, pico de gallo, and a squeeze of lime.

NOTES

- *If you're serving a mix of vegans, vegetarians, and omnivores, fry the oyster mushrooms first, then the fish. This helps keep the oil cleaner for the plant-based crowd.*
- *For even cooking and easy taco assembly, cut the cod into thin strips before battering and frying.*

VOLCANES

Tortilla Volcanoes

I spent my teenage years in Monterrey, Mexico, a city with a completely different vibe and modus vivendi compared to Mexico City. It wasn't easy at first; I had a hard time adapting. But once I found my rhythm in the city, I fell in love with it. To this day, there's no place in Mexico I'd rather live.

The mountains are breathtaking, the people are some of the kindest I've ever met, and the food culture? One of my absolute favorites. It was in Monterrey where I learned to make volcanes, a staple at any carne asada gathering. Nothing fancy: just friends around the grill, tortillas, meat, beans, salsa, cheese, and, of course, cold beers.

Volcanes are made by placing corn tortillas directly on the grill or griddle and leaving them untouched while delicious cheese melts over them. They are the perfect combination between a tostada and a taco. The tortillas crisp up beautifully, creating the perfect base for your favorite toppings—salsas, avocado, or whatever you have on hand. They're incredibly simple to make and truly a dream to eat.

SERVES 4 TO 6

- 12 corn tortillas (homemade, page 40, or store-bought)
- 1½ cups refried beans (any kind—pinto, black, homemade, page 37, or canned) or Frijoles Puercos (page 136)
- 1½ to 2 cups shredded cheese (like Oaxaca, mozzarella, or vegan cheese)
- Salsa of choice (see Los Básicos The Basics chapter for ideas)
- Avocado

Optional Toppings

- Crumbled vegan or regular chorizo
- Carne asada, grilled portobello, or Mushroom Carnitas (page 145)
- Grilled nopales or any other vegetable
- Pickled red onions, cilantro, jalapeños, lime wedges for garnish

Preheat a comal, cast-iron skillet, or griddle over medium heat. You can also make the volcanes directly over the grill.

Place the corn tortillas on the hot surface in a single layer, working one at a time, or as many as fit without overlapping. Let them warm for 30 to 60 seconds.

Spread a spoonful of refried beans evenly over each tortilla, then sprinkle cheese on top.

Cook, undisturbed, for 5 to 7 minutes, until the cheese is fully melted and the bottom of the tortilla is crisp and golden.

Remove from the heat, top with salsa, avocado, and your favorite toppings, and serve immediately.

PASTA CON SALSA DE CHILE ANCHO EN CAMA DE RICOTTA CON HIERBAS FRESCAS

Rigatoni with Ancho Chile Tomato Sauce, Whipped Ricotta, and Herbs

My love for pasta runs deep. There's just something about a good tomato-based pasta—the umami, the depth of flavor, and how incredibly simple it is to pull together a delicious meal.

Back when my kids played high school soccer, team dinners were a big deal. Every time it was my turn to host, they all requested pasta with tomato sauce. Word got out that it was *really* good, and by the end of the school year, I was making more and more, sometimes up to 6 pounds of pasta. Crazy, right?

This isn't the exact recipe I made for those dinners, but it *is* for all the pasta lovers out there—especially the ones who love a Mexican twist. Think of it as a beautiful mash-up of my two favorite cuisines: a rich tomato sauce layered with ancho chile and sun-dried tomatoes, tossed with short pasta, and served over herby ricotta. It's comforting, flavorful, and just the kind of meal that brings everyone to the table.

SERVES 6

1 pound rigatoni or other short pasta

4 tablespoons olive oil

6 garlic cloves, thinly sliced

½ cup diced onion

2 tablespoons ground chile ancho

¼ cup sun-dried tomatoes packed in oil, finely chopped

1 (28-ounce) can whole peeled San Marzano tomatoes, crushed

1 tablespoon kosher salt, plus more as needed

1 (15-ounce) container ricotta cheese or almond ricotta

Zest and juice of ½ lemon

3 tablespoons chopped fresh thyme, parsley, or basil, or a combination

Freshly grated Parmesan cheese, for serving

Bring a large pot of salted water to a boil. Cook the rigatoni according to the package instructions until it is al dente. Reserve about 1 cup of pasta water before draining.

In a large pot, heat the olive oil over medium heat. Add the garlic and onion and sauté until golden. Add the chile ancho and let it release its aroma, 20 to 30 seconds. Stir in the sun-dried tomatoes and cook for an additional 1 to 2 minutes, until they are softened. Add the crushed tomatoes and season with 1 tablespoon of salt. Simmer gently for 5 to 7 minutes.

In a food processor or a large bowl with a whisk, whip the ricotta. Season with lemon zest and juice, salt to taste, and the fresh herbs. Spoon the ricotta into a pasta platter.

Spoon the rigatoni into the sauce to coat. If the sauce is too thick, gradually add the pasta water, little by little, until it reaches the desired consistency. Serve the pasta on top of the whipped ricotta. Finish with freshly grated Parmesan cheese.

NOTE

- *This is a chunky sauce, but if you are more of a smooth sauce kind of person, you can always use an immersion blender to blend until creamy.*

SOBREMESA

SMALL SWEET BITES

Sobremesa is one of my favorite parts of any meal, the time spent lingering at the table, talking, laughing, and enjoying each other's company long after the plates are cleared. It's when stories are shared, life is caught up on, sometimes even business gets done. There's no rush, just connection.

In many homes, coffee, tea, or carajillos (espresso with Licor 43) are served, along with something small: nuts, sweets, or a tiny bite of dessert. I'll be honest: I'm not much of a dessert person. I'll almost always skip dessert in favor of an extra glass of wine. But little things to nibble on, or a flaky galette or empanada? Always a yes.

My favorite spread always includes a mix of nueces picosas, nueces garapiñadas, a few squares of dark chocolate, maybe some salty chips, just enough to keep the moment going. It's not about a big presentation, it's about the gesture. You're done with your coffee but suddenly craving something salty? The table's got you. Still sipping your wine and want a bite of chocolate? It's right there.

And if we're lucky, maybe sobremesa turns into round two. A few more botanas, reheated leftovers turned into tacos, another bottle of wine or a couple beers opened. It might sound a little chaotic, but that's the beauty of it.

That's the Mexican way—no se termina la comida, se alarga la vida.

GALETTE DE PIÑA

Pineapple Galette

The inspiration for this pineapple galette comes from two desserts I grew up eating—and loving.

The first one? Barritas de piña. A shortbread-style cookie filled with pineapple jam. It was amazing. Rectangular, with the jam peeking through the center and the edges folded just enough to hold it all together. That sweet-tart strip of jam running down the middle? Perfection.

The second? Pineapple empanadas dulces—a classic in Mexican bakeries. I always reached for those first.

And here's the twist life threw me: I married a pineapple farmer. Yes, my husband has a pineapple farm back in Mexico. So let's just say my love for pineapple has only grown over the years, literally and figuratively.

SERVES 6

For the dough

1¼ cups all-purpose flour

¼ teaspoon kosher salt

½ cup (1 stick) cold unsalted butter, cut into cubes

3 to 4 tablespoons ice water

For the filling

1 (20-ounce) can pineapple rings or chunks

3 tablespoons granulated sugar

1 teaspoon ground cinnamon

2 tablespoons flour or cornstarch

To finish

1 egg or 4 tablespoons coconut cream or plant-based milk plus 1 tablespoon maple syrup

2 tablespoons turbinado sugar

To make the dough, in a food processor, combine the flour, salt, and cold butter. Pulse until the mixture looks like coarse, wet sand. With the motor running on low, add 3 tablespoons of ice water. If the dough doesn't hold together when pinched, add 1 more tablespoon. Shape the dough into a disc, wrap in plastic wrap, and refrigerate until firm (at least 30 minutes).

Prepare the filling. Drain the canned pineapple well and pat it dry to avoid a soggy crust. In a bowl, toss the pineapple with the sugar, cinnamon, and flour. Set aside.

Preheat the oven to 400°F (200°C).

On a sheet of parchment paper or a silicone baking mat, roll the chilled dough into a 10- to 12-inch rough circle.

Using a slotted spoon or fork (to leave excess liquid behind), spoon the pineapple filling into the center, leaving a 1-inch border. With the help of the parchment or mat, gently fold the dough edges over the filling, pleating as you go. Leave the center exposed.

To finish, if using an egg, beat it. If using a plant-based option, mix the cream with the maple syrup. Brush the folded edges of the dough with your chosen mix and sprinkle with turbinado sugar.

Transfer the galette (still on the parchment) to a baking sheet. Bake for 30 to 35 minutes, until the crust is golden and the filling is bubbling. Let the galette cool slightly before slicing. Serve warm or at room temperature.

NOTE

- *Top with whipped cream, coconut whipped cream, or vanilla ice cream.*

NUECES GARAPIÑADAS

Candied Pecans

In the northern states of Mexico, you'll find the best pecans, and I mean *the best*. When I moved to Monterrey, I remember tasting the freshest, most delicious pecans of my life. Everywhere you turned, there were desserts made with nuts, or someone on the hunt for the *perfect* nueces garapiñadas (candied pecans).

Truth is, I never found "the perfect" one because there was always one more to try. And honestly? They were all amazing. That's the beauty of Mexican culture, so much creativity, so much flavor, always something new or different.

This is my go-to recipe for nueces garapiñadas. It's simple, classic, and to me, it's the perfect little bite to share during a long, good conversation over la sobremesa.

MAKES 2 CUPS

1 cup sugar (white or brown)

½ cup water

1 teaspoon ground cinnamon

1 teaspoon cayenne pepper, optional

½ teaspoon kosher salt

2 cups pecan halves or large pieces

In a large skillet or heavy-bottom saucepan, combine the sugar, water, cinnamon, cayenne pepper (if using), and salt. Heat over medium, stirring constantly, until the sugar dissolves.

Add the pecans and continue cooking, stirring constantly so they don't burn. Gradually, you'll see the liquid begin to thicken and turn into a caramel. Keep stirring until the liquid completely evaporates and the sugar crystallizes and sticks to the pecans (they'll look sandy).

Lower the heat and keep stirring for a few more minutes so the crystallized sugar slightly melts and forms a shiny coating around the pecans. Once golden and well-coated, remove from the heat and spread the nuts on a parchment-lined baking sheet or silicone mat. Separate them carefully so they don't stick together.

Let cool completely before storing in an airtight jar.

NOTE

- *You can replace pecans with walnuts, almonds, peanuts, cashews, or pumpkin seeds.*

MAZAPÁN DE PISTACHES

Pistachio Mazapán

Mexican mazapán is a soft, crumbly candy made from nuts and sugar. The most common is with peanuts. They usually come in round shapes, carefully wrapped in tissue paper to protect their delicate nature.

Sobremesa is the time spent after a meal, nibbling on a small treat, enjoying a digestif, a coffee, and long entertaining conversations. Mazapanes are a delightful dessert to enjoy during the sobremesa. You have to unwrap them carefully and savor each bite slowly and calmly, allowing your pace to match the rhythm of a relaxed conversation.

MAKES 6 TO 8 PIECES

1 cup unsalted dry-roasted pistachios

½ cup powdered sugar

Pinch of kosher salt

3 teaspoons tahini or pistachio butter

Place the pistachios, powdered sugar, and salt in a food processor fitted with the blade attachment. Blend until you have a sandy consistency. Pause the food processor occasionally to scrape the sides with a spatula. This might take 8 to 10 minutes.

Add the tahini and blend for an additional minute. The consistency should resemble wet sand; it should be slightly crumbly but stick together when squeezed between your fingers.

Shape the mazapán by pressing 2 tablespoons of the candy in a 2-inch round cookie cutter. Use the back of a spoon or a tart tamper to press the candy tightly. Carefully remove the cookie cutter to reveal a ½-inch-thick round mazapán.

Individually wrap each mazapán in a 6 x 6-inch piece of tissue paper. Store them in a tightly closed container in the pantry. They will be good for 1 week.

BESOS DE PISTACHE

Pistachio Kisses

These besos de pistache are a twist on a classic I grew up with, besos de nuez. But this time, I replaced the pecans with pistachios, and I'm not looking back.

There's something so delicate and special about pistachios—the flavor, the color, everything. These cookies are crumbly, just sweet enough, and perfect with a cup of coffee or as a little treat after lunch.

They're the kind of cookie that disappears fast and is ideal for gifting, sharing, or just keeping in a jar on your kitchen counter (if they last that long).

MAKES 32 COOKIES

1 cup shelled pistachios

2½ cups all-purpose flour

½ cup powdered sugar, plus 1 cup for dusting

Good pinch of kosher salt

1 cup (2 sticks) cold unsalted butter or vegan butter, cut into pieces

Preheat the oven to 350°F (180°C). Line a baking sheet with parchment paper.

Place the pistachios in the bowl of a food processor fitted with the blade attachment. Pulse until they reach a coarse, sandy texture similar to rough cornmeal. Be careful not to overprocess; you don't want a paste or pistachio butter.

Add the flour and pulse again just until everything is evenly combined. Next, add the powdered sugar and salt. Pulse a few times, then slowly add the butter, piece by piece.

Continue pulsing until the mixture looks crumbly and sandy. You're not looking for a smooth dough. The texture should resemble damp sand when you press it firmly in your hand, and it should hold together. Turn off the food processor and remove the blade.

Use a small ice cream scoop or cookie scoop to portion the dough evenly. This ensures all the cookies are the same size. Roll each portion into a ball, pressing them hard in your fist so they keep together, and place them on the prepared baking sheet.

Bake for 15 minutes, or until lightly golden on the bottoms and edges. Remove from the oven and let cool for 3 to 5 minutes.

While the cookies are still warm (but not hot), roll them gently in powdered sugar and place them on a platter or wire rack to cool completely. Test before storing; make sure they're fully cooled and set.

PASTISETAS

Butter Cookies with a Golden Bottom

I know, I know, what's a butter cookie doing in a Mexican cookbook? But hear me out.

There was this one brand of cookies, in a blue and white package, that felt *special*. In my grandma's house, those were the adult cookies. I still remember sneaking one, the browned bottom, that perfect crumbly texture.

Sure, we had Danish butter cookies and other fancy ones . . . but these? These were different. Crumbly, light, golden, not too sweet, just delicious. They stuck with me.

So, when I finally nailed the recipe, I knew I had to share it with you. Because some cookies are more than cookies—they're memories.

MAKES 24 TO 30 COOKIES

1 cup (2 sticks) unsalted butter, softened

¾ cup powdered sugar

1 teaspoon vanilla extract or paste

1½ cups all-purpose flour

¼ teaspoon kosher salt

Preheat the oven to 350°F (175°C). Line a baking sheet with parchment paper.

In a stand mixer using the paddle attachment, cream the butter and sugar until smooth. Add the vanilla and mix until completely integrated.

Gradually stir in the flour and salt until the dough comes together. It will be soft but not sticky. If it feels too soft, refrigerate it for 15 to 20 minutes. You can also work with half the dough and refrigerate the other half in the meantime.

Fit a pastry bag with a large star tip and fill it with the dough. Pipe 1-inch swirls onto the prepared baking sheet, leaving about 1 inch of space between each cookie. Hold the bag straight up and apply steady pressure to form tight, even spirals.

Place the cookies on the middle/lower rack of the oven and bake for 10 minutes or until the edges turn golden. Let the cookies cool on the baking sheet. Make sure they are completely cooled before storing them in an airtight container; if they are warm, they can become soggy.

NOTE

- *For a vegan option, I find that the Miyoko's or Flora brands of vegan butter work the best.*

OREJAS

Mexican Palmiers

Orejas are pan dulce classics you never forget and that all Mexicans grew up eating. Simple, elegant, and full of texture. Golden brown, buttery, and crackly with sugar, they're made with just puff pastry, cane sugar, and salt, caramelized deliciousness in every bite. They're the kind of treat that feels special even though they're incredibly easy to make. One sheet of puff pastry, a little sugar and salt, and you're in panadería heaven.

MAKES 16 TO 20 OREJAS

¼ cup granulated sugar

2 pinches of kosher salt

1 sheet puff pastry or vegan puff pastry, thawed but cold

Preheat the oven to 400°F (200°C). Line a baking sheet with parchment paper.

Sprinkle half of the sugar and a pinch of salt onto a clean surface. Lay the puff pastry on top and sprinkle with the remaining sugar and salt. Gently press the sugar into both sides of the dough.

Fold the two long edges toward the center so they meet in the middle. Fold once more to create a log with four layers. Chill for 5 to 10 minutes if too soft.

Slice into ½-inch-thick pieces and place them cut-side up on the baking sheet, spacing them apart.

Bake for 10 to 12 minutes. Rotate the baking sheet 180 degrees, then continue baking for 5 to 7 minutes more, until golden and crisp. Let cool completely; the cookies will continue to crisp as they cool.

NOTES

- *For a deeper caramel flavor, sprinkle extra sugar underneath each oreja before baking.*
- *Store in an airtight container at room temperature for up to 4 days.*

BEBIDAS

BEVERAGES

Mexican drinks range from homemade aguas frescas, which accompany meals, to sophisticated drinks. As a Mexican American, I enjoy honoring both my Mexican and American heritage by creating fusion combinations that represent both cultures. In this chapter, I include recipes ranging from timeless classics like limonada with chia, vampiros, and sangrita to modern aguas frescas like cherry hibiscus.

LA FAMOSA SANGRITA DE MI PAPÁ

My Dad's Famous Sangrita

What is sangrita? Sangrita (not to be confused with sangria) is a nonalcoholic drink traditionally served alongside tequila. It's meant to be sipped in alternation with tequila to enhance and complement the bold flavors of the agave spirit.

Now, here's the thing: This isn't just any sangrita recipe. This is *my dad's* famous sangrita, the one he's been making for years, and that always gets requested at family gatherings. When I set out to write it down, I had to call him and ask him *exactly* how he makes it. He laughed and said, "Ah, so you're finally ready for the recipe?" And just like that, the secret's out. Now it's here for the world to know.

That said, there's a twist. My version is inspired by his, but I've put my own little spin on it, and he was the first to tell me that's exactly how it should be. "Taste and adjust," he told me. "Make it your own." So that's my invitation to you, use this recipe as a guide, but tweak it to your taste. That's the heart of this drink: tradition with a personal touch.

MAKES ABOUT 6 SERVINGS

1 cup freshly squeezed orange juice

½ cup freshly squeezed lime juice

1 (5.5-ounce) can tomato juice (fresh or unsalted store-bought)

1 (11.5-ounce) can V8 original juice

2 teaspoons Tabasco hot sauce or any other, like Valentina or Cholula (adjust to taste)

2 teaspoons Maggi sauce

1 teaspoon Worcestershire sauce or vegan Worcestershire sauce

½ teaspoon salt

½ teaspoon freshly ground pepper or more to taste

Combine all the ingredients in a pitcher or jar.

Chill for at least 30 minutes so the flavors meld and it's nice and cold.

NOTES

- *Adjust the spiciness to your liking.*
- *Serve with orange slices and a side of chile salt or worm salt for a truly authentic experience.*
- *Serve in small glasses alongside a shot of blanco or reposado tequila or use as a base for other drinks.*

LEVANTA MUERTOS

Spicy Tomato Juice

When we lived in Mexico City, my family owned a weekend home in Cuernavaca Morelos. Due to its ideal climate, locals call this place La Eterna Primavera, or the eternal spring city. We had friends over for pool parties or carnes asadas, or hosted family for several days. No matter the occasion, weekends always felt like a party.

The day after some of these reunions or parties, my parents often prepared a large brunch featuring traditional Mexican dishes like guisados. My dad greeted our guests with his signature Levanta Muertos, a drink meant to "wake up the dead." We use this phrase in Mexico to describe the foods or beverages that cure hangovers after a night of drinking.

SERVES 2

4 tablespoons lime juice

1½ cups V8 juice or tomato juice

6 dashes of Maggi sauce

6 dashes of Tabasco sauce

1 (12-ounce) bottle Mexican lager

1 lime wedge, to rim the glass

2 teaspoons kosher salt

Ice

Place the lime juice, V8 juice, Maggi sauce, and Tabasco sauce in a medium pitcher. Carefully pour in the beer and mix. Taste. The flavor should have a tangy and salty taste, with a spicy finish in every sip.

To serve, rub the rim of a glass with a lime wedge. Next, place some salt on a saucer and dip the rim of the glass into it, rotating the glass until the entire rim is coated. Repeat this process with the other glass. Finally, add ice to the glasses and pour the Levanta Muertos.

CHELADAS

Prepared Beer with Lime and Salt

I'm convinced every Mexican kid grew up licking the rim of their parents' chelada glass. That tangy mix of lime, salt, and beer foam was weirdly irresistible and probably the first hint of how deep our love for salty, citrusy flavors runs.

Cheladas are simple: just beer, lime, and salt. But somehow, they taste like summer, like carne asadas, like Sundays with family. No frills, just refreshing, savory perfection in a glass. The kind of drink that makes you feel at home wherever you are.

MAKES 1

1 lime wedge, to rim the glass

Salt, for the rim

Juice of 1 lime

Ice, optional

1 (12-ounce) bottle Mexican lager (like Modelo, Pacífico, or Tecate)

Run a lime wedge around the rim of a tall glass and dip it in salt.

Fill the glass with ice if you wish, squeeze in the lime juice, and pour in the beer.

Stir gently and enjoy!

VAMPIRO

Tequila, Citrus, and Sangrita Cocktail

The vampiro is one of those drinks you'll often see at women's gatherings—baby showers, bridal showers, and casual get-togethers. Sweet, spicy, and bright red, it looks innocent . . . but don't be fooled.

There's a story that always makes me laugh from Monterrey, that my mom shares—*not all of Mexico, just Monterrey . . .*

When the vampiro started gaining popularity, many señoras thought it didn't have any alcohol. "Oh, it's delicious, like juice! But . . . I don't know why I am feeling uneasy," they'd say completely unaware that the splash of tequila or mezcal was perfectly hidden behind the sangrita, lime, and chile. A little too easy to drink . . . and definitely part of the fun.

MAKES 1

Chamoy, for the rim

Tajín, for the rim

Ice

1½ to 2 ounces tequila blanco

½ to 1 ounce lime juice

½ to ¾ cup My Dad's Famous Sangrita (page 180)

4 to 6 ounces grapefruit soda

Rim a glass with chamoy and Tajín.

Fill the glass with ice, then pour in the tequila, lime juice, and sangrita.

Top with grapefruit soda and stir gently.

NOTES

- *Glass size: A 16-ounce glass is ideal for serving one vampiro. It gives you enough room for ice, mixers, and all the garnishes without overflowing.*
- *Chamoy: My favorite chamoy brands are Mega Chamoy and Chamoy Tajín, both add the perfect balance of sweet, tangy, and spicy. Use them to rim the glass or even drizzle a little inside for extra flavor.*
- *Make it your own: Adjust the spiciness with more or less hot sauce, or swap the grapefruit soda for lime soda if you prefer it on the sweeter side.*

CARAJILLO SHAKEADO

Shaken Espresso

One of the things I love most about Spanish is how many words just *don't* have a real English translation. Like when you're wearing something for the first time, and someone asks if you're *estrenando*. Or when a dessert is so sweet it makes you stop mid-bite, and you say *me empalagó*. There's no exact word for that in English—and I love that we have one.

But then there are those moments when we do the opposite—we borrow English words, make them our own, and come up with gems like shakeado. You'll hear it at restaurants all over Mexico, especially when you order a carajillo. The server will ask, "¿Normal o shakeado?" and I swear, I'll never get over it. It cracks me up every time . . . and, yet, I always go for the shakeado. Obviously.

MAKES 1

Ice

1.5 ounces Licor 43

1 shot espresso (freshly brewed and cooled slightly)

Fill a cocktail shaker with ice. Add the Licor 43 and espresso. Shake vigorously for 20 to 30 seconds.

Strain into a rocks glass and serve with ice if you wish.

AGUA FRESCA

Mexican Fresh Fruit Drink

Aguas frescas are not just a pitcher of flavored water in your refrigerator. There's a whole world wrapped up in that simple jug.

Since I can remember, I could open *anyone's* refrigerator in Mexico and they'd say, "Hay agua fresca." For some families, it's always limeade. For others, it's hibiscus. But here's the truth: Aguas frescas aren't just a habit, they're a way of life. A way to use ripe fruit, a daily ritual, and a moment of creativity in the kitchen.

Got a bit of chopped melon left over from breakfast? Blend it with water and mint for the agua fresca para la comida. At my friend's house, there was always a pitcher of cherry-hibiscus agua fresca in the refrigerator. My parents usually had limeade or pineapple-mint. At my favorite restaurant? Strawberry-orange agua fresca that tastes like sunshine in a glass.

It all depends on what's in season and what's about to go bad. That's the beauty of it.

And if you've ever been to a paletería in Mexico, you know it's not just about paletas. There's usually a whole other section just for aguas frescas, with giant glass jugs lined up on the counter or inside the freezers. Watermelon, cucumber-lime, mango, tamarind, guayaba, strawberry, some with chopped fruit or milk in them, you name it. You can even mix flavors to make your perfect combo. It's a rainbow of options, and everyone has their favorite.

Aguas frescas are refreshing, yes, but they're also deeply personal. A little sip of home, no matter where you are, tradition, and whatever fruit life gave you that week.

Here's a great tip: If you have any leftover agua fresca, don't throw it away! Instead, turn it into paletas. Just pour the agua fresca into molds, freeze it, and you'll have the easiest homemade ice pops. You'll enjoy the same delicious flavor, but in frozen form. They're perfect for hot afternoons or as a sweet treat after dinner. In Mexico, we don't waste fruit; we transform it into something delightful.

On the following page, you'll find a guide to making aguas frescas along with some of my favorite recipes. Please use these recipes as a starting point and feel free to modify them to suit your taste. For instance, you might want to add more sugar, reduce the lime juice, or serve them with sparkling water, as my husband prefers.

Agua Fresca Formula

INGREDIENT	AMOUNT (FOR 1½ TO 2 LITERS / 6 TO 8 CUPS)	NOTES
RIPE FRUIT	2 to 3 cups, peeled and chopped	Use seasonal or slightly overripe fruit for deeper flavor and natural sweetness. In a pinch, use frozen fruit.
WATER	4 to 5 cups	Start with 4 cups and adjust to desired consistency after blending.
GRANULATED SUGAR	2 to 4 tablespoons	Taste and adjust—some fruits (like watermelon or mangoes) need very little.
FRESH LIME JUICE, OPTIONAL	2 to 3 tablespoons	Adds brightness and balance. Good for fruits like mango but not necessary.
FRESH HERBS, OPTIONAL	A small handful	Peppermint, spearmint, and basil blend beautifully with most fruits. Blend in or steep.
ICE	To serve	Alternatively, chill in the refrigerator until very cold.
OPTIONAL ADD-INS	Cucumber, hibiscus, ginger, chile, chia seeds, etc.	Great for layering flavor and using what you have on hand.

AGUA DE PIÑA CON MENTA

Pineapple-Mint Agua Fresca

MAKES ABOUT 8 CUPS

1 medium ripe pineapple, peeled and chopped

¼ cup granulated sugar (adjust to taste)

10 fresh spearmint leaves, plus more for garnish

6 cups cold water, divided

Ice, to serve

In a blender, combine the pineapple, sugar, mint leaves, and half the water. Blend until completely smooth.

Strain if desired. Pour into a large pitcher and stir in the remaining 3 cups of water.

Serve over ice and garnish with extra spearmint.

NOTE

- *In a pinch, fresh mint can be substituted for the spearmint.*

AGUA DE NARANJA Y FRESA

Strawberry and Orange Agua Fresca

MAKES ABOUT 5 CUPS

1 cup strawberries, hulled

1 to 2 tablespoons agave or granulated sugar, optional

3 cups cold water, divided

1 cup freshly squeezed orange juice

Ice, to serve

In a blender, combine the strawberries and agave (if using) with 1 cup of water and blend until smooth.

In a pitcher, combine the strawberry purée, orange juice, and remaining 2 cups of water.

Taste, chill, and serve over ice.

AGUA DE JAMAICA Y CEREZA

Cherry-Hibiscus Agua Fresca

MAKES ABOUT 6 CUPS

5 cups water, divided

½ cup dried hibiscus flowers (jamaica)

1 cup pitted frozen or fresh cherries

¼ cup granulated sugar (or to taste)

Ice, to serve

In a saucepan, bring 2 cups of water to a boil. Add the hibiscus flowers and steep for 10 minutes. Strain and let cool.

In a blender, combine the cherries with 1 cup of water and blend until smooth. Strain if you prefer a smoother texture.

Combine the hibiscus tea, cherry purée, remaining 2 cups of water, and sugar in a pitcher. Serve over ice.

LIMONADA CON CHÍA

Limeade with Chia Seeds

MAKES 4 CUPS

4 cups water

¼ cup granulated sugar, or to taste

½ cup freshly squeezed lime juice (4 to 6 medium to large limes)

1 to 2 tablespoons chia seeds

In a large pitcher, combine the water and sugar. Stir until the sugar is fully dissolved.

Add the lime juice and mix well. Taste and adjust sweetness or acidity as needed.

Stir in the chia seeds and let sit for 5 to 10 minutes, stirring occasionally, until the seeds begin to swell and form a gelatinous texture.

Serve chilled over ice. Stir before pouring, as the chia tends to settle at the bottom.

NOTES

- *For best results, use freshly squeezed lime juice—bottled won't give the same brightness.*
- *You can make it ahead: Store in the refrigerator for up to 2 days. Stir well before serving.*
- *Optional: Add a few mint leaves or a pinch of sea salt for a more complex flavor.*

ACKNOWLEDGMENTS

I like to say that Mexico holds my past, the United States shapes my present, and my future remains open to whatever it may bring. Living between two cultures and two languages has shaped not only how I cook, but how I see the world. This bicultural life has given me the experience, perspective, and flavor to accomplish one of my greatest dreams: writing this cookbook.

I know I am incredibly fortunate. I live a life that draws from the best of both worlds, and that gift has allowed me to turn my passion into my work. I am deeply grateful to the readers who have given my recipes a place in your kitchens and at your tables, and to those who, without even knowing me personally, trusted me enough to test the recipes for these pages. Your generosity, time, and trust mean more than you know.

Noel, thank you for testing the pistachio kisses. Maritzia, for trying the mango salad. Lucinda, for the pineapple galette. Elizabeth, for the egg tostadas. Agatha, for the enchiladas. Mel, can't believe you tested the garibaldi recipe at thirty-eight weeks pregnant! Thank you. Mau, hopefully you keep making the picadillo (with tomato sauce) for Valentina, and Daniel, the cortadillo for your kids. Gracias a los dos. Mami, ya quedó la torta de elote para hacerla una y otra vez. Roma, you are an expert in salsa verde now. Sofi, you make the best migas. Santi, I can't believe you tested the tinga recipe with zero tools. Serge, you are the best and most handsome macha salsa maker I have ever met.

Paloma, thank you, truly, for your honesty, your generosity with your time, and your willingness to work alongside me on this project. In my mind, there was no doubt that you were the only one whom I trusted the most for this. But above all, mil gracias por tu cariño y amistad durante tantos años. May this be the first of many, Palo.

Dianne Jacob, thank you for asking the hard questions and for squeezing my brain in all the right ways to make my book proposal so good. Because of you, I know I am a stronger recipe developer and storyteller.

Leslie Stocker, my agent, thank you for seeing my vision, believing in me, and trusting this project from the very beginning. Forever grateful.

Michelle Branson, thank you for your kindness, patience, and care through every round of edits. I will never forget to specify the size and type of onions again.

To the entire team at Gibbs Smith, you truly create beautiful books. I have not been able to wipe the smile off my face since I first saw the cover and layout. Thank you for bringing this dream to life, even more beautiful than I imagined.

Lee, thanks for always putting up with me and my crazy ideas, and for keeping the blogs up and running so well until I come and turn things around with a new one. I am still very sure that we will give our competitors a big scare, lol.

Mariana Velazquez, best food stylist ever, thank you for letting me pick your brain for this book. Your advice meant so much. Lorena Masso, gracias, gracias for organizing my mind before the photo shoot. You are one of my favorite food photographers, and I am certain we will work together soon. Sandra A. Gutiérrez, thank you for leading the way and opening space for Latin cookbook authors.

David, Eva, Matías, Valentina, I hope you have as much fun and as many mischievous moments around the table as I did growing up with your dads. Mau and Daniel, I have always said I never needed sisters because I have the best brothers in the world, and I still stand by it. Growing up, your companionship and complicity made every meal worth staying at the table until we were dismissed—even when I gave away half of my biscuit.

Sugero, thank you so much for opening your home and taking care of all the props I ordered, and, most of all, for showing us your willingness to live fully and enjoy life the way you do.

Mami, thank you for planting in us the idea of comer bonito: beautifully set tables, good manners, and the most delicious food. It is a gift that the three of us now share with our children, and that I have the privilege of sharing with so many people around the world.

Papi, imagine if you hadn't taught me how to make tablitas? This book might never have happened. Gracias. And above all, thank you for teaching us to "just do it," that discipline is freedom, and the only way to do things well (hacer las cosas bien).

Miko, I still miss you, buddy.

Santiago, Sofía, and Romina, you are my greatest gift y mi mas grande motor. The light and joy you carry reach farther than you know, and I could not be more proud of each one of you. Thank you for putting up with my recipe disasters, for celebrating the wins, for teaching me something new every day, and for being the best hand models ever. I love you more than you'll ever know.

Sergio, thank you for always believing in me more than I have believed in myself. You have a gift for seeing possibility where I or others see doubt, and for making everything and everyone better. I know I am better because I met you, because you always stand beside me, making me lighter, braver, and stronger every step of the way.

SOURCES

Anforа

ANFORA.COM/EN

This Mexican tableware company's porcelain dishes have been used in restaurants and homes across Mexico for generations. Known for their durability and simple, timeless design, their plates and bowls are a favorite for serving everything from soups and salsas to tacos and enchiladas.

Casa Chechen

CASA-CHECHEN.COM

Casa Chen carries a beautifully curated selection of Mexican pieces made by highly skilled artisans. Every item is thoughtfully chosen, highlighting the craftsmanship and tradition behind objects made by hand.

Crow Canyon Home Enamelware

CROWCANYONHOME.COM

Crow Canyon Home makes enamelware that truly makes me happy. The colors and patterns are beautiful, and their durability makes the pieces perfect for hosting, parties, and everyday meals when you want the table to feel fun and relaxed.

Earlywood

EARLYWOODDESIGNS.COM

Earlywood Designs creates some of the most beautiful and practical wooden kitchen tools. Each piece is thoughtfully made, durable, and designed to be used and loved every day in the kitchen.

La Chicharra

LACHICHARRACERAMICA.COM/EN-INT

La Chicharra Ceramics, from Oaxaca, creates beautiful handmade pottery that highlights the incredible craftsmanship of Mexican artisans. Their pieces feel special and full of character, the kind of ceramics that instantly make a table feel more beautiful.

Masienda

MASIENDA.COM

Masienda is dedicated to preserving and sharing the rich traditions of heirloom corn from Mexico. Their masa harina and tortilla making tools help home cooks experience the beauty and flavor of real nixtamalized corn.

INDEX

METRIC CONVERSION CHART

Volume Measurements

U.S.	Metric
1 teaspoon	5 ml
1 tablespoon	15 ml
¼ cup	60 ml
⅓ cup	75 ml
½ cup	125 ml
⅔ cup	150 ml
¾ cup	175 ml
1 cup	250 ml

Weight Measurements

U.S.	Metric
½ ounce	15 g
1 ounce	30 g
3 ounces	90 g
4 ounces	115 g
8 ounces	225 g
12 ounces	350 g
1 pound	450 g
2¼ pounds	1 kg

Temperature Conversion

Fahrenheit	Celsius
250°	120°
300°	150°
325°	160°
350°	180°
375°	190°
400°	200°
425°	220°
450°	230°

ABOUT THE AUTHOR

Alejandra Graf is the recipe developer, writer, and photographer behind AleCooks and Piloncillo&Vainilla, two bilingual food platforms dedicated to plant-forward, flavor-driven cooking inspired by Mexican and global traditions. Born and raised in Mexico, she brings together the warmth of home cooking with practical, modern recipes designed for everyday life.

Alejandra has spent more than a decade creating approachable dishes that help families eat more vegetables without sacrificing comfort or flavor. Her cooking style is rooted in real life—busy schedules, mixed dietary preferences, and the belief that good food should bring everyone to the table.

When she's not in the kitchen, she's usually with her family—eating, lingering over a good sobremesa, and stretching meals into conversation. And when she finds a quiet moment alone, she loves to read, go for a run, or play with her dog, Paco. This book reflects her philosophy: cook with intention, keep it flavorful, and always make room at the table for everyone.